"Near Dublin"
& Belfast
& Cobh

The Story of Laurel and Hardy in Ireland

Liam Muldowney

"Near Dublin"

The Story of Laurel and Hardy in Ireland

First published 2019

©Liam Muldowney

ISBN #: 978-0-244-75603-1

The photographs reproduced in this publication are done so with the permission of the owners, and none may be copied, reproduced or used without their prior permission. All efforts to contact the copyright owners have been made. If a reproduction is listed or credited incorrectly, all efforts will be made to correct this for future publications.

This book is sold subject to the condition that it shall not be lent, resold, hired or otherwise circulated without the publisher's prior consent in any form of binding cover other than that in which it is published and without a similar condition this condition being imposed on the subsequent purchaser.

Some of the photographs are reproduced directly from newspaper prints as original negatives were unavailable. Apologies are made for the quality of these photographs deemed too important to omit. Photograph enhancements by Colin Howe.

For My Dad Billy

Who introduced me to Stan and Ollie.

He didn't see Laurel and Hardy live at The Olympia.

He did see

The Beatles live at The Adelphi!

(That's almost as cool)

Acknowledgements

A publication like this would never have been possible without the help of the following people and organisations.

Members of the Sons of the Desert worldwide, The Jitterbugs Tent Ireland, Colin Howe, Sean Dowling, Tom Copperthwaite, Steve O'Connor, Roger Robinson, John Ullah, Mandy Finney, Eric Woods, Gary Winstanley, Alison Stevenson, Richard Bann, John Carpenter, Randy Skrevedt, Trevor Dorman, The Wilson Photograph Collection, Wilson's Pharmacy Cobh, Alex Kane, Gerry Dunne, Keith Davidson, Holgi Dorr, Harry Hoppe, Neville Wiltshire, Stephen Bond, Mrs. Callie Connolly, Aidan Cruise, Antony and Joanne Mitchell Waite, Andreas Baum, Nico Cartenstadt, Bernie Hogya, Noeleen and Frank Reid, Victor Coe, The Gresham Hotel, The Royal Marine Hotel, The Shelbourne Hotel, Hunter's Hotel, Mount Usher Gardens, lettersfromstan.com, Helen and Billy Muldowney, Dave Tomlinson, RTE, Rootsweb, Tim Moriarty at the Irish Railway Record Society, Old Belfast Facebook, Eoin McVey at The Irish Times, www.irishnewspaperarchives.com.

To "The Other Monkey" Stephen O'Crowley, Jitterbugs Tent Vice-Sheik who edited the manuscript (so if you find any spelling mistakes, call him) and also gave up his lunch breaks to annoy the hotels of Dublin and ask questions of their unsuspecting staff. His support, research, enthusiasm and friendship has been more helpful than he will ever know.

All efforts have been made to give due credit for each photograph used in this publication. Where a copyright holder has not been found or contact has not been made, and issues copyright to a photograph, edits will be made for future editions. No copyright infringement is intended. All letters written by Stan Laurel are reproduced as he wrote them and come courtesy of www.lettersfromstan.com.

My wife Trudi and children Sarah, Emma, Billy, Aoife and Tommy who have been on this Stan and Ollie journey with me for many years. I think they've enjoyed it and I'm certain that by their laughter, they have also enjoyed the films.

Finally to Stan Laurel and Oliver Hardy who made over 100 appearances on the big screen in an effort to bring laughter and smiles to a weary world, I thank you. I thank you for coming to Ireland and bringing your joy to so many.

Contents

Introduction ... 7

Early Hollywood and the Irish ... 12

The 1940s ... 24

Let's go to Europe ... 33

Chant du Cygne ... 38

The 1952 Tour ... 45

The Support Acts ... 74

Belfast ... 101

Here We Go Again (1953) ... 121

Saps and Colleens at Sea ... 124

Cobh ... 130

Dun Laoghaire ... 152

The Supporting Acts ... 184

Jean Darling ... 198

Oliver Hardy's Irish Roots ... 202

The Rest of the Story ... 207

Introduction

Ballinteer, South of Dublin, 1974. ("South of what Suh?") Nine years since the passing of Stan Laurel. Seventeen years since the passing of Oliver Hardy. Five years since the birth of Liam Muldowney.

Irish television consisted of one channel that was RTE1. Some houses had enormous towering aerials on their roofs that enabled them to receive a snowy picture from the west coast of Wales, onto the massive television sets in the living rooms of Dublin and the east coast. For those who had a few shillings extra each month, a subscription to the new phenomenon that was "RTE Relays" would bring early cable TV into your home and the far better signal that led to BBC1 and BBC2 and not forgetting Ulster Television's UTV.

With BBC2 came Laurel and Hardy and this is my earliest memory of seeing these two men in their black and white films. I am going to say that "Busy Bodies" was the first L&H film that had scenes that I remember. From then on I wanted more. Two men doing silly things. Silly things and getting away with it. Friends who stuck together. Friends who made silly mistakes that I could not believe they made. Silly mistakes that made me laugh. Made me laugh and feel good afterwards.

I was only four or five years old and they were on in the afternoon just before dinner time. Dad would arrive home from work and we'd quickly usher him to his armchair so that the three boys and single girl as it was at that time (another would arrive later), would sit wherever we could find a free spot and watch magic unfold on the screen. The smell of whatever was cooking came from the kitchen and I think that my mother's maternal duties were the cause of her missing some of the best family time I ever remember and so wish I could experience again. But at least we were well fed.

I recall being insanely jealous of my older brother's Larry Harmon edition Laurel and Hardy annual. I have since thankfully managed to acquire it. (Well he did move out first)! There were Laurel and Hardy face puppets and Laurel and Hardy comics. A Laurel and Hardy mirror hung on our landing for years (I acquired that too). They featured heavily in our house.

Dad told me they were on in the cinema when he was a kid. "Fillers", he called them. Played before the main feature to "fill" the time. "Sometimes we went for the Laurel and Hardy's more than the main feature", he said.

When I was seven or eight, myself and a school friend who shall remain nameless (Ronan), put on a little Laurel and Hardy show for the entire class which involved us lying on the floor as if in bed, and an annoying telephone that kept ringing. I played Ollie and watched as Ronan (sorry, Stan) answered the phone. "You don't say. You don't say. You don't say", he said. When he came back to me I asked, in my best haughty Oliver Hardy tone, "who was it?" Ronan (Stan) looked at me and with a silly Stan grin said, "He didn't say!" We didn't win the prize but we still remember doing it. Thanks Ro.... I mean Stan!

The release of the Vision Videos Laurel and Hardy collection in the mid-1990s pumped new life into their films as satellite television began to flood our screens offering too many channels, too much choice and not enough classic comedy. The address of Rob Lewis's Tent of the Laurel and Hardy Appreciation Society on the reverse of every video prompted me to send a letter to see if there was an Irish chapter.

Rob's early guidance and help was the start of the Jitterbugs Tent Oasis#220. There had been a Tent in Belfast and a tent in Cork but one man Tents were now outlawed by this comedy society.

I wanted a working Tent, something that would last and be an outlet for members to come and enjoy the Boys on the big screen. I had arrived on the scene when things were changing for the Sons of the Desert. Exhausted Ruler John McCabe had ruled that each Tent must have five subscribers to the Intra Tent Journal. I placed an ad in Rob's Laurel and Hardy Magazine and within weeks had the five subscribers we needed. I applied and the great Dwain Smith replied and sent me our charter.

Foundered on April 1st 1999, The Jitterbugs Tent Ireland was born. Those early years were scary as we didn't make enough door money to cover room hire costs. We got there with the sheer determination to succeed and bring the Boys to as many people as we could. I received letters of support from other Tents and Sons who wished us well and offered support. I almost shook in horror when Alison Grimmer, editor of the Intra Tent Journal in Europe told me she was coming to one of our early meetings. I need not have shook. She came over and my family still regard her as a very special friend.

At the time of writing we are in our twentieth year we are stronger than ever and striving to get better and better. We hosted the 8th European Convention in 2007 and bizarrely enough it was our first convention. But it wasn't just us. We had help and advice from all corners and it was a collective convention. I recall Mandy Finney saying to me at the end of it all that, "You guys got it just right".

Laurel and Hardy is as much a state of mind as a comedy duo. The Sons of the Desert is a family and a friendship ring. We are special people. I have never felt anything else like the Sons of the Desert feel good factor in my life.

This book is for all Sons. I was asked to write something like this many times but resisted, believing that there just wouldn't be enough source material. What I collected over the last twenty years needed to be shared. The final ask came from the great Roger Robinson. He came to Waterville in County Kerry to support the Jitterbugs Tent as we took a Laurel and Hardy museum to the annual Charlie Chaplin Film Festival. I presented a small show on the visits of Laurel and Hardy to Ireland. Afterwards, the usually placid Roger turned to me and quite forcibly said, "There is a book in that. Write it now." (No chance of him saying, "It's my round, what are you having?")

My family have "not seen me" apparently, whilst I've been writing it. My work wife Debbie, who knows a little about Laurel and Hardy, has had to listen to me getting excited about writing it.

Finally last, but very much not least, Jitterbugs Vice-Sheik, Stephen O'Crowley who has had to put up with daily WhatsApp messages asking advice, guidance and more delving into his research. Our Scooby Doo moment is something I will never forget (you will read about it later). This is as much his research as mine and it would not have happened without him. I thank him and as our wives are fond of saying, "If he ever left me it would be for him".

Laurel and Hardy came to Ireland on two occasions. Their intention was to make people happy. They exceeded this and left memories in people's hearts and lives that still exist today. To them and their support acts, we thank you.

This is primarily a reference publication and is the result of twenty years collecting stories, newspaper articles, photographs and archive hunting. It lay in files and in boxes and it would have been shameful to leave it there and not share it.

If I could turn back the clock to 1952, just for two hours, I'd buy you all one of these and we would be able to experience the magic of Laurel and Hardy in Dublin.

Early Hollywood and the Irish

It could be argued that both Mack Sennett and Hal Roach, two of Hollywood's pioneering film studio owners were well ahead of their time. Both managed to spot and nurture talent and both had an uncanny head for comedy and seeing the gag in every possible situation.

Sennett's Keystone studios gave many stars their grounding in movies including Mabel Normand, Marie Dressler, Harold Lloyd, Roscoe Arbuckle and Harry Langdon. His Keystone Cops delighted many audiences around the world with their fast paced zany comedy style, a style that Sennett used to great effect.

Sennett and an official of the New York Motion Picture Company saw a young British comedian onstage in New York and recognised his potential for film comedy. A telegram was duly sent to Mr. Alf Reeves, Tour Manager with the Fred Karno Touring Company asking that a,

"Chaffin, or something, make contact at once with Kessel and Baumann, 24 Long Acre Building, Broadway."

Arriving at the building and seeing it was mostly inhabited by Attorneys, Charles Chaplin's initial thought was that his Great Aunt Elizabeth Wiggins had died and left him an inheritance. He was disappointed to find out that they wanted him to sign with the Keystone Company as a comedian. However disappointed he was, sign he did and the rest is movie history.

Roach too had an eye for talent. Having worked in the movie industry as an extra, he used an inheritance to fund his studio dream. Along with his friend Harold Lloyd, they produced the Lonesome Luke comedies which some would argue rivalled and were in fact quite similar to the Chaplin films. Expansion followed and Roach produced some of the most popular comedies at the time, including those starring Will Rogers, Max Davidson, Charley Chase and of course the Our Gang Kids.

In 1927 one of Roach's directors Leo McCarey who had been watching two actors work together, suggested that they be teamed as they complimented each other really well. This pairing of Laurel and Hardy would prove to be a momentous achievement for the Hal Roach Studios.

Of course much of what came out of the studio was down to its owner's policy of allowing carte blanche to directors and actors when it came to filming. The "Lot of Fun" as it came to be known had a reputation for being an amazing place to work, and a happy workforce creates fantastic work.

Both of these studio owners were of Irish stock. Roach born in New York and Sennett in Quebec, were both grandsons of Irish immigrants. Coincidental? Perhaps. The Irish are known around the world for their love of a party and a good time. A good Irish sense of humour and an eye for a joke and a gag could have contributed to the working lives of these pioneers. However we have to look at the Ireland that their grandparents came from. Hardly a barrel of laughs or a basis for comedy, or was it.

Sennett was born in 1880 and Roach in 1892. Take an average of a thirty year period for a generation and it's easy to see that both grandparents would have possibly left a country during one of its worst periods in history, the Potato Famine (1845-1852), where the population was reduced by up to twenty five percent. Emigration was rampant from a country where the majority of its people relied extremely heavily on the potato as a main source of food. The working classes were hit hardest. Reports stated that people were dying on the roads and were buried in mass graves. The sorry state of the Irish farmer and his children was written about in the newspapers. People literally begging for a right to food and a right to survive lead to the extremeness of eating grass and leaving one's home and family to try and desperately find a new life in the new world. Not a great base for comedy geniuses but the Irish resolve probably shone through.

As the masses took the boats and hoped that they might survive the journey, they stuck together. They looked out for each other, helping in whatever way they could. Communities built up and families of like stayed together. Irish areas in the great American cities ensured that the children of immigrants would always know of their heritage. Nights full of storytelling and singing kept the resolve of the Irish strong and that filtered down through the generations thus keeping alive the Irish spirit in the new world.

Mack Sennett was the son of John Sinnott, son of an Irish immigrant from County Wexford who settled in Quebec. John married Catherine Foy in a Catholic ceremony in 1879 and when Mack (Michael) was seventeen they moved to Connecticut, along with another son George. During his teenage years Michael was known to have been proud of his Irishness. He wrestled with his idea of a typical Irish man, hardworking and hard drinking and also with his dreams of becoming a professional entertainer and singer, something his mother encouraged him to follow.

Far less is known of Hal Roach's family apart from the fact that he too was a grandson of Irish immigrants. His grandfather John Roach was a hugely prosperous man and before the civil war owned a plantation adjacent to that of General Robert E. Lee of the Confederacy. The United States Pentagon stands there today. Hal Eugene Roach (sometimes preferring just Eugene) made the trip to the old homeland on a number of occasions. On one of these occasions he purchased several Roach family crests which he was very proud of. Indeed he made no secret that both he and Mack Sennett were extremely proud of their heritage and that they had Irish blood in their veins.

Both men encouraged their teams with very different styles. Sennett's worked from the ground up, stripping everything back to a very bare rawness that was almost cartoon like. Ladies were heroines, there to be simple and rescued. The men were heroes, ready to jump at a chance to impress a fair maiden, whilst the villainous rogue was a heavily moustached, top hat wearing blaggard.

The characters might fall from cliffs, get run over by speeding vehicles or even crushed beneath huge boulders, but they seldom got injured or died. There is certainly a hint of Irishness in this style of impossible humour which at times had been called the lowest form of comedy.

Hal Roach on the other hand preferred a more sophisticated style of comedy. Well written and well thought out, his characters did get injured and the black eyes and bandaged limbs showed this. It was more believable and allowed the watcher to engage more with the character. The "Lot of Fun" was full of happy employees, and friends and relatives of those employees also worked at the studios.

The happy working nature of the studios showed in the films it produced which were full of charm and feeling. It was said that you could cry at a good Roach comedy and that's a difficult thing to do.

Michael "Mack" Sennett

Hal Eugene Roach

In 1913 Sennett directed Roscoe Arbuckle and Mabel Normand in "The Riot". Arbuckle plays a stereotypical Jewish businessman who falls foul of a couple of Irish children who open a package of expensive clothing being delivered by a young girl. He takes offence and has words with the leader of the Irish community, played by Charles Inslee. The two sides descend into an all-out war that starts with brick throwing and punching, quickly ending up with bombs replacing the bricks. The Keystone Cops are well out of their depth and have to call in the services of bayonet charging militia. IMDB describes the two sides as being "clearly on ethnic lines".

Described by The Moving Picture World as, **"a full reel given over to a free-for-all fight, in which bricks and bombs are thrown. A race war ensues and the situations contain a lot of harmless amusement free from vulgarity."**

Appearing in an uncredited role as one of the cops is Edgar Kennedy, himself of Irish descent and later a perfect foil for Laurel and Hardy, most notably in their 1930 short "Night Owls", where Edgar plays an obvious Irish policeman trying to get into the chiefs good books.

Brick throwing and fighting it seemed were something of an Irish stereotype in early Hollywood as we can see in one of Hal Roach's Irish efforts over a decade later.

In 1924, Roach produced a comedy starring Stan Laurel. "Near Dublin" went against the usual style of comedy for a Laurel film. Roach employee H. M. Walker described it as "not being up to the others" that Stan had recently made. However, Motion Picture News described it as "well produced and affording Stan Laurel one of the best and most loved comedies he has had for quite some time." They also described it as "a travesty on the well-known Irish plays that will undoubtedly register big."

Drawing on the "Oirish" stereotype, the film has a marriage arrangement in exchange for a debt right off, a village dance in which a fight breaks out, a murder and a trial and eventually a couple running away with a sheriff chasing after them in a dancing manner. Just your typical day in an Irish village.

Motion Picture World described it as "a type of romantic Irish play. It is amusing and the plot and atmosphere are quite out of the ordinary."

The film was well received, probably within the larger Irish diaspora and it is a wonder that the format and subject matter weren't used more. It survives today and is well worth watching for its slapstick and over emphasised Irish costumes and characters.

Also worth noting in the film is the appearance of James Kellie (also known as Jimmie Kelly), who played the part of Judge Jim Kelly! James was an actual Irishman being born in 1854 in Castlebar, Co. Mayo. He had appeared in numerous Chaplin shorts between 1915 and 1918 including "A Night at the Show", "The Floorwalker", "The Pawnshop" and "Easy Street". Kelly also appeared with Harold Lloyd in possibly his most famous film, "Safety Last". He ended his film career at the Hal Roach studios and his appearance in "Near Dublin" is very entertaining as he attempts to drink his drink that has been spiked by Stan Laurel who is hiding in the hayloft and is now having a great time disrupting the court proceedings.

Irish born James Kellie in "Near Dublin"

James Kellie wasn't the only Irish born actor who made their mark in silent comedy films. A number of others are worth noting and amongst them was Kate Price.

Left, Kate Price

Born Katherine Duffy in 1872 in Blackpool, County Cork, she was quite a prolific silent film actress appearing in over 300 films with such greats as Mary Pickford, Roscoe Arbuckle, Snub Pollard, Douglas Fairbanks Jnr. and Buster Keaton. One of her more famous roles was the part of Keaton's accidental wife in his 1922 short "My Wife's Relations".

Of huge importance to Laurel and Hardy fans is the fact that while Kate worked at Vim in Florida, she made a number of shorts with Oliver Hardy who was sometimes billed as "Babe". This attempt to produce a comedy team was mildly successful but ended when the Vim Studios did, in early 1917.

Kate Price is probably best known for her role as Mrs. Kelly in the Universal Pictures series, "The Cohens and The Kellys", the story of two feuding families and the hilarity that ensued. It lasted a total of just six films but they were hugely popular.

Kate retired in 1937 and died six years later aged 70 at the Motion Picture Country Home. She is buried in Calvary Cemetery.

Buster Keaton and Kate Price in a scene from "My Wife's Relations".

Another Irish born actor is Creighton Hale. Born Patrick Fitzgerald in Cork in 1889, he was educated in Dublin and London before joining a troupe of actors and heading off to the United States. He was spotted by the Pathé Company who offered him work in front of the camera. He changed his name to Creighton Hale and worked with D.W. Griffith who used him as comic relief in several films. He was well known as a leading man in the 1920s starring in "The Cat and The Canary" and "Broken Hearts of Broadway" with Coleen Moore. He appeared with Thelma Todd in "Seven Footprints to Satan" in 1929 and also made appearances in Our Gang shorts including "School's Out" and "Freewheeling". Worthy of note is his name being linked to an early porn movie in which he was said to have starred. The rumour lasted years before it was established that he did not in fact appear in it. (It's worth looking up just for the sheer bizarreness of the plot, but not for inclusion here).

Oliver Hardy and Creighton Hale in "Should Men Walk Home" 1927.

The coming of sound saw him slip out of demand for leading roles and he spent the next thirty years as an uncredited extra in movies such as "The Maltese Falcon" and "Casablanca". He died in 1965 in California.

The list could go on and include the Moore Brothers, Rex Ingram, Mary Pickford and many others who left a mark in those early Hollywood films. However a silent comedy film star with Irish roots who has to be included is Paddy McGuire (sometimes Maguire). With seventy four credits as an actor between 1915 and 1920, he was best known for playing the stereotypical Irishman, drunk, rowdy and up for a laugh at all costs.

Beginning his career with Chaplin at Essanay, he worked as a supporting actor for a number of studios, mostly playing a character called Paddy Maguire, strangely enough! Worthy of note is his appearance in "Heaven Will Protect a Woiking Goil", where the movie ends with Paddy and his villainous cohorts driving into a huge chasm and walking away unhurt. The last line of the film goes to Paddy who simply says, "Let's go and get a drink."

Chaplin, Paddy McGuire and Ernest Van Pelt in The Tramp 1915

Paddy died in died on 16 November 1923 in Norwalk, California, supposedly of insanity.

Paddy McGuire, Charles Chaplin, Lloyd Bacon, Edna Purviance, and Ernest Van Pelt in "A Jitney Elopement" (1915)

The 1940s

The story of the lives and film careers of Stan Laurel and Oliver Hardy has been extremely well documented over the years. Numerous books and essays have been carefully researched and written about this comedy duo who simply broke the mould when it came to screen comedy. Without doubt their movies have touched lives, brought laughter and good humour to the world and no one could argue the fact that their mark has well and truly been left. Stan was once asked what comedy was and I have often wondered about his response.

"How the hell do I know? I just know how to make people laugh."

A great response from a comedy genius or an abrupt answer to a stupid question? I pondered this for years until I didn't decide on an option, I knew which option it was. An abrupt answer to a stupid question. It is understandable perhaps why a person would ask the question but *why* would you ask one of the world's greatest comedians a question like that? His art is making people laugh through actions and words, not analysing those people and their response to actions and words. We are all different. Different people laugh at different things. What one finds humorous another will not. Take for example a person slipping and falling over in the street. It's the thing that slapstick films used with great effect. In reality half of the population will laugh and find that funny while the other half will ask if the person hurt themselves and is ok? Add cuts, bruises and blood and suddenly almost all of the population will be asking is that person ok? But slapstick movies did not have cuts, bruises and blood and as remarked in the previous chapter, they seldom got injured. So it is funny in that instance. But analysing all of this is overthinking and that was not for Stan.

Stan's art was in taking a scenario and twisting it in whatever way he possibly could to drain it of all the laughter. That was Stan's genius. He understood what worked. He knew whether a gag would work or not. But not only that, Stan Laurel was a master when it came to realising how good a gag was and how far he could push it. Buster Keaton knew this and said as much at Stan's funeral.

"Chaplin wasn't the funniest. I wasn't the funniest. Stan was the funniest."

Why would another legend of the silent comedy era comment like that? When Stan died in 1965, Buster Keaton was enjoying something of a revival. His short films were being shown on television once more. He was in high demand for television adverts and appearances on shows such as Candid Camera, where his deadpan, straight-faced look was used to very funny ends. He knew his star was once more shining and yet he adulated Stan Laurel to the top.

Buster Keaton was also a genius. He knew that his genre of comedy and Chaplin's genre of comedy was different to Stan's. Both Keaton and Chaplin appealed to a lot of people and those people flocked to see their films. Stan Laurel appealed to the masses and his comedy attracted a wider audience. Buster was basing his comments on the fact that people smiled and enjoyed Keaton and Chaplin films, but people laughed out loud at Stan Laurel films.

Having spent three decades making movies that made audiences laugh out loud, Stan Laurel and Oliver Hardy found themselves outside the gates of the Hal Roach studios since they first began their partnership. During the years 1941 to 1945 they made eight more movies, six for 20th Century Fox and two for M.G.M. A lot of Laurel and Hardy fans would agree that these movies were poorly made and possibly should never have been made. Working for the bigger studios meant following stringent rules. They were given scripts that had to be followed by the book and no matter how much Stan protested and tried to make them better and more suited to their style, he was not allowed to alter the shoot. Budgets and time sheets had to be followed and the freedom that Stan had enjoyed at the Roach Studio was not to be found.

It has been suggested that the Fox studios tried to suit their style more so than M.G.M. by pairing them with directors and teams that worked with them and were suited to the Laurel and Hardy way. But these films lacked the old sparkle and pace that the Roach films were abundantly full of. The gags were slow and the storylines were sometimes padded with the odd love interest and side story that did not even involve Stan and Ollie.

They were also getting old and it showed in the slower pace of those 1940s movies. There was less falling into lakes and down holes, more than likely due to their age and their abilities Add to the fact that Universal's new team of Abbott and Costello were topping box offices everywhere and suddenly Laurel and Hardy were very out of fashion.

As is the way of life, their finances began to grow smaller. Whilst at Roach, the Boys were paid actors. Very well paid actors. At one point during their time there a year's pay for Stan was $135,000, $88,600 for Oliver and $129,000 for Hal Roach. They were very highly paid actors. Stan received more than Oliver due to his writing, directing and editing the films, something Oliver did not want to be involved in and he was quite alright with the money difference. Stan did more of the work so why shouldn't he get paid more? Sadly there was a trade-off. They did not own the rights or have any ownership of any of their films, something that Chaplin and Harold Lloyd did have. Both of those men ended up quite well off during their retirement years.

There were divorces and with divorces come alimony payments. Stan in particular fared quite badly due to this. Their lawyer and friend Ben Shipman was quite a talented man at keeping Stan out of huge alimony strife and managed to save him a lot of money by making sound legal arguments on his behalf. Shipman was the studio lawyer for Roach and eventually became Business Manager for them both as well as their business partner in their company Laurel and Hardy Feature Productions. Shipman also negotiated their contracts with both M.G.M. and Fox and it was after their last movie for Fox that work dried up. And when work isn't there and money runs out decisions have to be made.

The next decision they made involved a man who would be providing the vast majority of their work for the rest of their lives.

British theatre promoter Bernard Delfont approached them with an offer of a U.K. stage tour.

Bernard Delfont was born in the Crimea in 1909 but the family moved to the east end of London in 1912. He left school at twelve and followed his brother Louis into music hall. He changed his name to Delfont and formed a double act with comic Hal Monty and they billed themselves as The Delfont Boys. His last stage appearance was in 1937 and in 1949 he started in theatre management and acquired a series of theatres in the West End. He joined forces with the impresario Val Parnell and as a result was able to buy the lease on the Prince of Wales Theatre and to stage many of his shows at The Palladium.

He moved into television becoming stage producer for the BBC summer season variety show, "Carefee". From there he moved to ITV and was instrumental in producing a host of variety shows including, "Bernard Delfont Presents" and "Bernard Delfont's Sunday Show". The Royal Variety Performance was allowed to be televised in 1960 and it soon became the major television event to be associated with Delfont. The following year The Royal Variety Performance was presented by

Delfont, under his "personal supervision".

He was instrumental in getting Eric Morecambe and Ernie Wise to sign for ITV for their first series. He became one of the most powerful men in television and was knighted in 1974. Two years later he was made Baron Delfont of Stepney.

He was well known in show business for his personal generosity and was much involved with charitable causes. He was a former president of *The Variety Club of Great Britain*, life president of *The Entertainment Artistes Benevolent Fund*, and president of the *Entertainment Charities Fund* from 1983 to 1991. He died on 28 July 1994.

Although initially anxious about their reception in the music halls of Great Britain, Stan and Oliver accepted Delfont's offer mainly due to the lack of any other.

Their anxiousness need not have been an issue as they arrived in Southampton on 11th February 1947 to hordes of waiting cameramen, and cheering crowds. They had reworked an old stage sketch of theirs called "The Driver's Licence" that Stan had written for them to perform at a Red Cross benefit in 1940. They opened on February 24th in Newcastle. Audiences were given the Stan and Ollie experience that began with the Boys walking onto the stage, which itself generated howls of laughter. As Ollie tries to welcome everybody to the show he is constantly interrupted by Stan who eventually tells Ollie that he was, "standing on my foot!"

The main bulk of the sketch involves Ollie trying to renew a driving licence that he originally inherited from his grandfather! In giving his name as Oliver N. Hardy, it turns out that the N. stands for Enry. "You don't write Henry with an N," suggests the Cop and Stan replies, "Of course you don't. You write it with a pencil."

The sketch continues with gags about their recent change of address due to them not being able to raise the rent and the fact that Ollie has a driving conviction for speeding, on the pavement. There were visual gags involving Ollie's cane and Stan's finger that has a splint on it. At one point the splint ends up on Ollie's finger and the Cop ends up being slapped in the face as Stan tries to retrieve it. They help themselves to the contents of the Cop's lunchbox and it all ends with chaos as they are chased off stage by the Cop who has reached for his shotgun.

The sketch had audiences howling with laughter and was considered a great success.

On Friday 21st March the boys took time out and travelled down to Kent where they had been invited to open a section of the Romney Hythe and Dymchurch railway. A section of the railway that travelled to Dungeness had been closed during the war years and used primarily for military service. Now it was to be re-opened to the public and the Boys seized the chance to break their routine for the day.

Train Driver Tony Baker doesn't look too worried as Stan and Ollie hijack his train. Courtesy of Roger Robinson.

It was pure Laurel and Hardy comedy as they took the oversized key and used it to great effect by messing up the opening of the main tunnel door that they were supposed to open. Newsreel footage exists of the event and it is obvious that the huge crowd in attendance were thoroughly enjoying this live improvised Laurel and Hardy show.

The winter of 1947 was one of the coldest that the country had experienced for many years and the beginning of the tour was not the most enjoyable for Stan and Oliver. However the summer months more than made up for it especially on one warm June evening when Stan met up for a reunion with his father A.J. Jefferson and sister Olga at the pub she managed with her husband Bill Healy, The Plough Inn in Grantham.

Stan and his father A.J., Ida Laurel behind Stan with Bill Healy. Olga behind Oliver. Courtesy of Dave Tomlinson.

The Boys performed up and down the length of the U.K. until the end of September when Oliver Hardy's visa expired. They were having fun performing each night and decided not to return home just yet. Very hastily, a tour of Europe was planned and Laurel and Hardy set sail for the continent.

Sadly the tour did not include any Irish dates.

"Let's Go To Europe"

The first port of call was Denmark where performances were arranged in Copenhagen, Aarhus and Odense. Once more they found themselves mobbed at train stations and in the streets, such was their popularity. In Denmark, they were known as Gøg og Gokke. Sons of the Desert member Roger Robinson visited the Palace Hotel in Copenhagen and was delighted to see the guest book contained not only their names but their Danish names too.

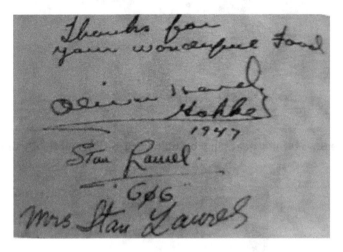

By kind permission from Roger Robinson (a swell guy).

It was on to Sweden next and performances in Stockholm, Gothenberg and Malmo. The Boys then headed back to Denmark where they were welcomed at Copenhagen City Hall by a U.S. Government official and the Chief Mayor, before making a few hastily arranged personal appearances including a visit to a famous brewery. Surely the stuff of diplomats and royalty, not Hollywood movie stars, but such was their status. They appeared at a charity benefit that evening at the Ambassadeur Restaurant in aid of "Save the Children". The Boys also made a radio broadcast of their stage sketch which included the audience whistling along to the Cuckoo song.

The Boys turning heads in Stockholm. Courtesy of Leif Dahlstrom.

Signing the visitor's book at a Danish Brewery.

Drinking Carlsberg, who don't make comedy teams but if they did, they would probably be the best comedy team in the world!

The Boys in Copenhagen. Courtesy of Pia Bondesson

From Denmark the Boys took the train to France and had just enough time to catch their breath before beginning a six week run at the Lido de Paris. There was a brief interruption to the Paris shows when they took a trip back to England where they had been asked to appear on the Royal Variety Performance at the Palladium in London.

Who could refuse such an offer? Laurel and Hardy took to the stage in front of King George VI, Queen Elizabeth, Princess Elizabeth and her fiancé Philip Mountbatten and also Princess Margaret. The royal romance added to the occasion and indeed the couple were married two weeks later.

Appearing alongside Stan and Ollie were Gracie Fields, Tommy Trinder and Eva May Wong amongst others. Afterwards, the King commented that he had not laughed so much in years.

The Boys in Paris clowning around to the delight of the crowd.

The Boys returned to complete their Paris shows and then travelled to Belgium where they spent two weeks in Brussels before performing in five different towns within the space of a one week. On the 8th January 1948 Laurel and Hardy finally finished their tour in Ghent and returned home to America.

8th January 1948, Laurel and Hardy in Ghent, Hélène Maréchal, one of Belgium's most famous stage stars is the woman in the middle of the picture welcoming the Boys to the city.

"Chant du Cygne"

The story of Laurel and Hardy's movie swansong "Atoll K", has been told many times and makes for an interesting chapter in almost all the biographies on the pair. Writer Norbert Aping penned a complete book on the saga (The Final Film of Laurel and Hardy), and the entire mess that surrounded the filming of this chaotic production could itself be the subject of a movie. The plot of the film is readily available and copies of it on DVD and Blu-ray are also easy to obtain so I won't touch on it here. The story behind the film's production is important however especially in the context of their later tours and should be told.

By 1950 the American audiences viewed Laurel and Hardy as a part of movie history. Abbott and Costello were topping the box office with each eagerly awaited release and Dean Martin and Jerry Lewis were just beginning their run of success. A new generation of Americans were growing up and Stan and Ollie were not part of their lives. Television was beginning to be the new phenomenon in entertainment but the old Laurel and Hardy shorts were not on the listings just yet.

In Europe however they were still monstrously famous and idolised. George Bookbinder, an American financier realised this. Post war Europe was a dreary place and morale was quite low. Rationing was still part of the lives of the hard working population and there was a general feeling that the world had nothing to smile about. Most experts agreed that one way to boost morale was through the entertainment industry and cinema was top of the list. The French, Italian and British governments were all keen to use cinema as much as possible and home grown film was a way in which this could be achieved. The governments provided financial grants and low tax systems for the industry in a bid to kick start and inject new enthusiasm into locally produced film.

Bookbinder knew that a film starring Laurel and Hardy would be a huge box office hit and he set about making this a reality by hiring a man named Deutchmeister who was contracted to Universalia Produzione in Rome. Two French companies, Franco-London films and Films E.G.E. signed on the dotted line to obtain distribution rights with Les Films Sirius of France, Fortezza Films in Italy and International in the U.K. What could possibly go wrong?

When approached with the idea of starring in an independent film, filmed in France with no big studio interference, Stan was interested. Due to government grants, the money was very good and the estimated twelve week shoot was something that was extremely appealing. Bookbinder contacted agent Paul Kohner who, upon hearing it was a Laurel and Hardy film, employed his brother Frederick and his writing partner Albert Mannheimer. Mannheimer accepted another job just prior to beginning the film and was replaced by a friend of Oliver Hardy, John Klorer.

Both Kohner and Klorer were told that they would be the principal writers but having arrived in Paris, the Americans realised that they were part of a team that also consisted of Frenchman Rene Wheeler and Italian Pierro Tellini. Again, what could possibly go wrong?

Klorer spoke English, Wheeler spoke French, Tellini spoke a little French and also Italian. Kohner spoke French and English. All in all it was beginning to sound like a Laurel and Hardy scene in itself.

Money was no object and elaborate hotels and villas were hired for the writers. After a number of weeks there was still no script. Stan and his wife Ida arrived in Paris in April 1950 and Stan was ready to get working on expanding the script. With none available, he was told he would just have to wait. After another number of weeks Kohner was simply enjoying the Paris hospitality at the expense of the governments realising that working as part of that team of four was fruitless.

By June, it looked like the bare bones of a script was ready and upon hearing this, Oliver Hardy and his wife Lucille made the trip to France. They were greeted by Stan and crowds of cheering French fans, some wearing Stan Laurel masks. With no time for resting, they were taken on a promotional tour of Italy to publicise the film that was not yet even written.

Finally Kohner and Klorer were able to take a script to Stan at his hotel, the George V. Stan was eager to get reading and asked both men how it was. They replied that it might need a bit more work and Stan suggested that every script needs a bit more work. Kohner remarked years later that he knew Stan would not like it. "It was awful."

Next day, they returned to the hotel to meet with Stan and found him very agitated. He could not believe that they had spent three months working on it and asked them if they really expected him to accept "this rubbish."

"This rubbish", was about to get worse.

Stan tried to understand the script as best he could, working tirelessly, attempting to inject some sort of sense into it. He asked Monty Collins. An old friend and gag-man to help. Two famous European comedians were due to be part of the cast for the movie but French comic

Fernandel and Italian clown Toto pulled out of any association with the production having made up their minds that it was ill-fated. Also at the last minute the director Tim Whelan was replaced by Leo Joannon who had actually contributed the original story idea for the film.

French actress Suzy Delair was signed to appear and when shooting finally began France was hit with a terrific heatwave which was to provide difficult conditions for the entire shoot. On the first day of shooting the initial scene took three hours to set up and Joannon wanted Stan and Ollie to rehearse. The boys were having none of it and argued back that they knew exactly what to do. Humouring them, the director agreed to allow them shoot the scene unrehearsed and was left completely amazed at their professionalism and how they managed to get it shot perfectly in one take.

The supporting actors spoke in different languages. Producers and directors spoke in different languages. Filming was a chaotic experience for everyone. Stan asked for help from his pal Alf Goulding. Goulding obliged but resentment from the French and Italian crew ensured they undermined everything he did.

Oliver Hardy was having trouble with the heat. His heart was a cause for concern when it developed an irregular beat. At this time of his life he was at his heaviest and he had lost most of his gracefulness and light footedness. Stan too had issues. He developed dysentery from the food cooked in the on-site catering cars. He lost a lot of weight and then developed prostate problems. He was treated in the American Hospital in Paris and Ida Laurel acted as both nurse and translator for him. He also had to contend with diabetes, having developed it in 1949.

When Stan returned to the shoot a makeshift hospital had to be erected on set and he could only work for thirty minutes each day, needing much rest in between. In the completed film Stan at times looks very ill and his appearance detracts from whatever chance "Atoll K" had of being even remotely funny.

Stan bemoaned the fact in later life that due to the movie being shot completely out of sequence, a lot of his gags were not used. Many years later he was of the opinion that there were a lot of funny moments that could have been written into it to make it a better production.

Filming finally ended and the two comedians returned to the United States in April 1951, a full year after Stan had initially arrived. The twelve week shoot had turned into twelve months. It was released in various formats and at different times around the world between 1951 and 1954. Versions of the film differed from ninety eight minutes to eighty two minutes and it was released as "Robinson Crusoeland" and "Utopia" in certain countries.

Its tenure was brief and Stan was pleased the film disappeared from cinemas quite quickly. There are moments of classic Laurel and Hardy but as a whole it does not work. Whilst receiving a poor rating on all levels, there are some Laurel and Hardy fans who will speak positively of the film and support it.

In Ireland in was released in 1952 as "Robinson Crusoeland".

Coincidentally it was on release at exactly the time that Stan Laurel and Oliver Hardy were on a two week engagement at Dublin's Olympia theatre. So it might be said that Dublin was the Laurel and Hardy capital of the world.

As a final nail in the coffin, a copyright blunder meant that the film was never registered and so to this day it remains in the public domain and is probably the most widely available Laurel and Hardy film.

Above, a screen grab from "Atoll K" showing how ill Stan looked. The exhaustion also shows on Oliver's face.

Two cinema stills from the Irish release of "Atoll K", "Robinson Crusoeland" The back of the stills are stamped; "E.J. Fancey Productions (Ireland) Ltd. 102 Middle Abbey Street Dublin". From the author's collection.

The 1952 Tour

Stan recovered well back at home and was soon ready to work again. When Bernard Delfont offered them another tour of Great Britain's theatres the two comedians jumped at the chance. Having enjoyed the previous tour so much and with the memories of a disastrous experience making their last film still quite raw, it was a welcome offer.

They were to travel once more in the company of their wives Ida and Lucille and due to travelling together and staying at the same hotels, their friendship had taken a new turn since the 1947 tour and the experience of Atoll K. During their heyday they had retained a working relationship. There had been dinners and parties at their respective homes but that was as far as socialising with each other went. Oliver had his friends at the golf course and the race track and he was also a Mason. Stan on the other hand was a workaholic, preferring to spend his time at the studio working on gags and in the editing room. So with the enjoyment of the last tour and their new level of friendship, this was probably a time of great excitement. And this tour included dates in Dublin and Belfast. Laurel and Hardy were finally coming to Ireland.

Stan and Ollie arrive in Southampton to be greeted by a couple of Hula Girls.

Taken from newsreel footage.

They arrived at Southampton on the Queen Mary on 28th January 1952. Also on board was the British Prime Minister Winston Churchill. Having spent a number of days on board it is highly likely that these two men met. Given Churchill's love of comedy films and his previous visit to the Chaplin studios, the conversation must have been intriguing. The Boys were greeted by two girls wearing grass skirts in an obvious play on their movie Sons of the Desert. There is an awkward moment when Stan rubs a finger on the arm of one of the girls and then licks it. She ponders for a moment and then takes a backward swerve as if in shock. Stan doesn't notice this and hands a lollipop to each girl with the other girl giving him a big hug causing him to react with his trademark cry before making a hasty retreat.

The next four weeks were spent rehearsing their sketch, "A Spot of Trouble". Stan wrote the sketch specifically for the tour and enjoyed performing it at the time. Later in life he became unhappy with it in its entirety and even went as far as destroying his own personal copy thinking it would be lost forever and never seen again. Thankfully his daughter Lois found a copy during the late 1980s and it was reproduced in albeit a shortened version, in John McCabe's book, "The Comedy World of Stan Laurel".

Basically the plot involves the Boys on a deserted railway station. They pass each other several times before finally seeing one another. There are no trains and they decide to sleep on the only bench that is there. Much is made of the fact that Ollie is very large and there is obviously not enough room for Stan. A policeman arrives and is about to arrest them for vagrancy but instead involves them in a plot to get him into his chief's good books. They have to break in to the chief's house and get arrested by the cop! Simple.

The scene on the bench was taken from their films "Berth Marks" and "Pardon Us". In both of those films the Boys have trouble sharing a particularly small sleeping area. The entire story of the cop coming up with an idea to get into his chief's good books was taken from their film "Night Owls". Also throughout the sketch there are lines and gags used from the films "Pack Up Your Troubles" and "Way Out West" and why not. Stan more than likely wrote these sketches and gags in the first place and they did make for extremely funny watching. Audiences wanted to see classic Stan and Ollie and if there were some familiar scenes it definitely added to the enjoyment. Compare it to going to see a concert by your favourite singer and they did not play all the hits you loved so much but instead only played new material. It certainly would not be as enjoyable.

Laurel and Hardy opened on February 25th at the Embassy in Peterborough. There were a few disappointing reviews in the local newspapers but the audiences did not care. Packed houses showed just how much the Boys were loved and for the next two months they played to full houses the length and breadth of Great Britain.

On April 13th they left their hotel in Nottingham and were driven to Bottesford to the Bull Inn where Stan's sister Olga was the Landlady. She had closed the pub to her customers in order to treat her brother and his wife, along with the Hardy's, to an English roast dinner and some quiet time.

Stan, Oliver, Bill Healy, Stan's brother in law and Stan's sister Olga

On 23rd May 1952, Stan wrote to his friend Booth Coleman from the Empire Theatre in Liverpool.

"All here as usual - looking forward to Dublin - leave Hollyhead - Sunday night - arrive Monday a.m. but don't open till Tuesday - due to not being able to scenery & props in time for Monday show - so will have a chance to look around a bit. Will drop you a line from there in Gaelic."

Stan

The tour continued and having completed their engagement in Liverpool they took the overnight ferry to Dublin on Sunday 25th May and went directly to the Gresham Hotel on O'Connell Street.

The Gresham Hotel had been witness to a host of important events in Ireland's history. It was founded by Thomas Gresham who was named after the founder of the Royal Exchange in London where he had been abandoned as a baby, (he was found on the steps). He made his way to Dublin as a young man and gained employment as a butler to an aristocratic family. In 1817 he left his job and purchased 21-22 Sackville Street, now O'Connell Street. How he obtained the finances to do this remains a mystery. For almost fifty years he operated as a lodging house, catering for wealthy members of the British parliament who were passing through Dublin on their way to London. The hotel was badly damaged during the Irish Civil War but was renovated to a very high standard and remains a top Dublin hotel to this day.

The Gresham Hotel and O'Connell Street, Dublin around the time the Boys stayed there.

Above, the hotel in 2019. Courtesy Stephen O'Crowley.

The next morning a reporter from the Daily Mail wrote that both had missed breakfast and did not appear until noon. He noted that Stan **"looked every inch like that little man who got his partner into every conceivable mess."** The reporter was shocked to hear Stan speak in a deeper and quieter tone than the high pitched screen voice he was used to and **"although he did not have much to say, he said it in a shy and charming way. Oliver Hardy on the other hand loomed larger in life than he does on screen and he still sports his tiny moustache."**

There was a chance to have a little more rest as a mix up meant that their scenery would not arrive until the following day. As a result, opening night on the 26th May had to be cancelled.

Laurel and Hardy were booked to play two weeks at Dublin's Olympia Theatre on Dame Street in the centre of the city. The theatre itself was built to very specific instructions by John J. Callaghan, a prolific architect from the mid to late 1800s. Callaghan was employed by the great Dan Lowery who wanted to bring his business to Ireland having successfully built up a music hall empire in the U.K. He made it a personal ambition to do so. His primary instructions were that it was not to be a theatre, licensed premises, eating house or dwelling house. It was to be a combination of all of them.

It opened its doors for the first time on 22nd December 1889 as "The Star of Erin" to enormous success. Lines of people ran along the streets outside trying to gain entrance. The spacious bars and lavishly decorated rooms were a sight to behold. The day after opening night however, the police entered the venue and arrested Lowery for selling alcohol in a part of the premises that he was not supposed to.

It was renamed "Dan Lowery's Music Hall" in 1881 and again renamed "Dan Lowery's Palace of Varieties" in 1889.

In 1897 the Lowery family were no longer in ownership and the venue opened as a theatre and renamed "The Empire Palace". It hosted the Fred Karno comedians on many occasions from this time right through to the 1920s. Karno's "Mumming Birds" was performed more than once as adverts from the national newspapers show. This of course was the show that Charles Chaplin and Stan Laurel appeared in and try as I might, I cannot be absolutely sure that either man came to Dublin at this time although it is highly likely that they did.

Sons of the Desert pretending to be royalty in one of the elaborate boxes at the Olympia Theatre on the occasion of the 2007 Sons of the Desert European Convention. Courtesy of Stephen O'Crowley

In 1923 the venue became "The Olympia Theatre" and it remains so to this day. It changed hands in 1952 when it was purchased by Stanley Illsely and Leo McCabe, both well known in Dublin's theatre circles. It was they who promoted Laurel and Hardy in Ireland.

A recent investment of over €4 Million has resulted in major upgrades to all four bars as well as new seating and the addition of extra shops in the Stalls and Circle areas. The theatre has never looked better.

Exterior of The Olympia Theatre as it looks today with its stained glass façade. Courtesy of Stephen O'Crowley

Laurel and Hardy took the extra day off gladly and chose to relax in their hotel. A reporter from The Irish Independent found them sitting in the foyer minding their own business. During the conversation he had with them they expressed how impressed they were at the warmth of the welcome they received in Dublin and that they wanted to make plans to return to the city for a vacation and possibly see some more of the country. The reporter noted that Hardy was the more serious but still very amiable member of the team whilst Laurel portrayed a lively sense of fun. When asked if they would be making any more pictures Oliver Hardy replied, "Yes, but only if we can make them as we want them."

"Hardy who now weighs 22 stone was once a keen golfer but gave it up during the war. "Give him a paint brush to do odd jobs around the house and he is happy", added Mrs. Hardy. Laurel's hobby is deep sea fishing but there was a twinkle in his eye when he heard about the price-tagged perch in Poulaphouca Lake."

Evening Herald press photo, apologies for the quality.
www.irishnewspaperarchives.com

Film Comedians' Visit

Laurel and Hardy pose in Dublin.

www.irishnewspaperarchives.com

OPENING NEXT TUESDAY
FOR TWO WEEKS
Nightly, 6.45 and 8.45.
MATINEES (FIRST WEEK ONLY):
Wednesday and Saturday at 3.
ILLSLEY-McCABE
announce the first Irish appearance of

LAUREL
AND
HARDY
Booking is VERY Heavy!
PRICES : STALLS, 6/6; CIRCLE, 4/-
Booking above attractions, 10.30 to 6

Opening night began on Tuesday 27th May and The Dublin Times reported:

"What Laurel & Hardy have to say to each other doesn't matter. They merely have to appear on stage and the house rocks, shrieks and hoots with laughter. Much of the laughter came from children, but their parents were spellbound too."

The Daily Mail reported,

"A howl of laughter greeted Laurel and Hardy as they walked on stage at the Olympia theatre, looking exactly as they do in all their films. The laughter came from the adult members of the audience who had been fans for twenty five years and were obviously delighted to see all their old mannerisms and facial expressions brought so wonderfully to life before their eyes. Their act is ideal for children of all ages containing the maximum of slapstick but it has a very special appeal for those who have been faithful followers and will, therefore, recognise many of the scenes. There is not enough of them but the time they are with us is filled with laughter."

The Evening Herald saw it as the following,

"On to the stage strode a little man wearing a broad benign grin, a pair of big baggy trousers, and a battered bowler, carrying what once upon a time might have been a respectful looking violin case. The crowd roared with delight only to break into a howl of mirth a moment later when he was followed by a somewhat large gentleman, with a worried countenance and a gleam in his eye that spelled trouble for the little man with the benign grin. Yes, it was Dublin's welcome for those famous comedians Laurel and Hardy."

The Irish Press reviewed it a little differently,

"At the Olympia last night, O'Laurel and O'Hardy, as they called themselves, presented a weak sketch and put the stage stuff over by force of their personalities. It was just as well that the Dublin audiences cheered their appearances as the noise drowned the somewhat feeble dialogue of the comedy effort called, "A Spot of Trouble." It is a pity that the presence of the comic pair alone is supposed to make one's journey to the Olympia really necessary. If the management wants them to stay for some time, something more in conformity with their uproarious film displays might be in order." R. J.

The Irish Press of Wednesday May 28th noted: ...

"Mr. O'Laurel and Mr. O'Hardy were the latest distinguished visitors to Dublin. In private life they don't make you laugh ha-ha, but they do make you smile. "I have always believed" Oliver Hardy said to me yesterday, "I know more about pictures than Stan does, because I am bigger. If I listened to him I wouldn't fall over as many cliffs or things like that, but I'm sure I know more about pictures.""

Reporter Mac Alla was in their hotel room when the phone rang ... "

It was somebody saying that he had been told to contact Laurel & Hardy and he got onto Stan. The context wasn't clear, but they were to get in touch with somebody. The somebody couldn't get in touch with them, because the somebody hadn't turned up. Chaos all around. "You should have hung up before he did," said Oliver sitting majestically in his chair. "I didn't know he hung up," said Stan "I wasn't listening...."

Stan's hobby is deep-sea fishing and he boasted about the tuna he caught weighing 258 pounds, which he landed in 44 minutes. Oliver had won before the war 172 cups for golf. He played off a 7 handicap. Bob Hope, Bing Crosby and John McCormack were among his frequent opponents. "I liked John best, he couldn't go too fast" said Oliver. "He played a nice slow game. So did I." Oliver has now taken up gardening, starting with a 3-acre garden.

Their favourite pictures of the ones they made are "Fra Diavolo", "Bonnie Scotland" and "Babes in Toyland".

Mac Alla then asked them if they were going to meet anybody important while they were in Dublin.

"Everybody is important to us" was the joint answer. Mrs. Hardy went on to describe her husband as a great handyman around the house, just give him a paintbrush and he is happy."

He finished his article by saying, "Give him a paintbrush anytime and the audience is happy".

Edain, a reporter from The Irish Press was invited to join the Boys at a tea party in their dressing room after the show one night. He reported that

"Oliver Hardy was under threat of putting on weight on the tour due to eating out so much. The climb backstage, escorted by Stanley Illsley and Leo McCabe to their dressing room however was helping counteract this threat. This pair of comedians are a real tonic, in spite of the fact that Oliver Hardy has a problem that worries him not little but quite much. He just can't find out from what part of Ireland his grandmother Mary Tomkin emigrated a hundred years or so ago. Granted the Genealogical Office is only across the road from the Olympia Theatre, but every time he has tried to make his way there, autograph hunters impede progress, almost to the extent of creating a traffic jam. *(For more information on this story and on Oliver's grandmother, see page 202).*

Their wives are with them on this, their first trip to Ireland. A nice pair of sensible women who enjoy travelling and share their husbands' liking for cups and cups of tea. Mrs. Hardy was a continuity girl and script writer in film studios and after twelve years of matrimony still thinks Oliver is wonderful. 'The handiest man you could have around the house and a real good garden furniture maker.'

What they like here are the enthusiastic audiences and the air of friendliness. So much so they intend taking a week off next month, hiring a car and driving around the country. On the other hand Oliver feels that if we want to attract tourists, the price of meals in hotel restaurants might well be reduced. Two pounds eighteen shillings he and his wife paid for a meal consisting of one fillet steak, one portion of liver and bacon, asparagus for two and strawberries and cream for two."

Interesting how Oliver commented about the high cost of restaurant food when he ordered fillet steak, possibly the most expensive item on the menu! Also noted is the appearance of strawberries on his menu. In the 1950s and right up until the early 2000s, the strawberry season in Ireland consisted of a few weeks in mid-summer. Oliver would have paid quite heavily for his strawberries which would have been imported from abroad at that time of the year and as a result would have been a hefty price. Something he may not have realised coming as he did from Los Angeles where strawberries were available all year round.

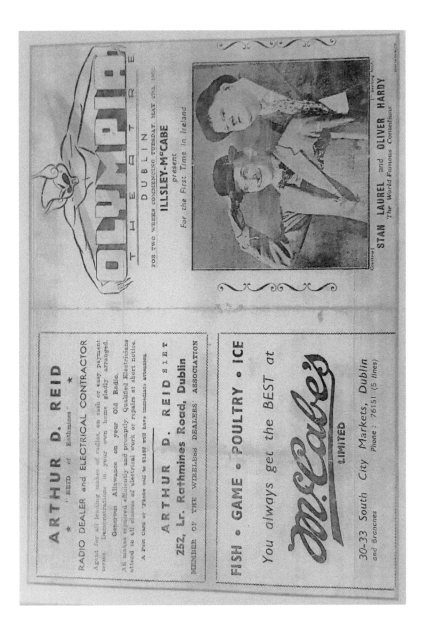

Garden Tools

*

Lawn Mowers

*

Kitchen Equipment

*

T. LENEHAN & CO. LTD.

IRONMONGERS

124/5 Capel St.

Jameson

RINGS

40 HENRY STREET AND 33 LR. O'CONNELL ST. DUBLIN

★ AFTER THE SHOW IT'S *Paradiso* TIME ★

★ THERE IS A WELCOME WAITING FOR YOU
DELICIOUS FOOD AND DRINK "*And Music Too*" ★

Open : 9.30 a.m. to 2 a.m. Weekdays ★ Noon to Midnight Sundays

Restaurant Paradiso 32 Westmoreland St.

(Adjoining "Irish Times")

★ SNACKS, GRILLS, LUNCHEONS, TEAS, OUR PASTRIES A SPECIALITY

Programme

Two Performances nightly at 6.45 and 8.45 p.m.

1. OVERTURE. ROBERT BOLTON and the OLYMPIA THEATRE ORCHESTRA.
2. The LONSDALE SISTERS. "Rhythm."
3. LORRAINE. The Singing Cartoonist.
4. The Sensational AERIAL KENWAYS.
5. ARCHIE ELRAY and Company in Ventriloquial Scena.
6. The GREAT CINGALEE and his company of skilled Mystifiers. "The Silent Man of Mystery" in Oriental Magic.
7. *INTERVAL* Musical Interlude : Olympia Theatre Orchestra.
8. The LONSDALE SISTERS.
9. JIMMIE ELLIOT. Famous Animal Mimic, of Radio.
10. MACKENZIE REID and DOROTHY. Ace Accordionists.
11. ILLSLEY-McCABE present, by arrangement with Bernard Delfont,

STAN LAUREL *and* **OLIVER HARDY**

— IN —

"A SPOT OF TROUBLE"

A Comedy Sketch in Two Scenes.

LOCALE : *A Small Town in the U.S.A.*

Scene 1. Waiting Room at the Railway Station.

Scene 2. The Chief of Police's Living-room.

CAST :

Officer (A Small town cop with a mind smaller than the town) Leslie Spurling

Chief of Police .... Kenneth Henry

Two Gentlemen En Route STAN LAUREL and OLIVER HARDY

NATIONAL ANTHEM.

STAGE MANAGER	For the Olympia Theatre Limited	HERBERT CARROLL
MUSICAL DIRECTOR		ROBERT BOLTON
CHIEF ELECTRICIAN		FRED BEASLEY

This Theatre is Disinfected throughout with Jeyes' Fluid

WHELANS
SOUTH KING STREET

Beside Gaiety Theatre. King 77975.
Popular TUITION DANCES—Mon., Wed., Fri., Sat., Sun., 8—11.30
Absolute Beginners and Improvers catered for. (Refreshments)
Tango Foxtrot Classes, Tues., 8—11.
FRANK and VERA M. WHELAN,
Fellows I.S.T.D., N.A.T.D. (former also Examiner A.I.B.B.D.)
Why not try our six or twelve Private Lessons' Course ?
Sufficient for Social Purposes
CAFE OPEN 10.30 a.m.—6.30 p.m.

COMMODORE
TYPEWRITERS

Office Models from £49 10s 0d
Portable, with Carrying Case £27 10s 0d
SOLE AGENT IN IRELAND
BRYAN S. RYAN
91 HARCOURT STREET, DUBLIN
TELEPHONE : 53884, 53889, 53933.

SKEFFINGTON LIMITED

*

The Confectioners

*

68 DAME ST., DUBLIN AND BRANCHES

Ice Cream Manufacturers
As Served in this Theatre
Suppliers to some of the Leading Hotels and Theatres in Dublin

*

ENQUIRIES INVITED
TELEPHONE No. 46286

For all your sports goods

Hely's OF DAME STREET

Backstage at the Olympia theatre with promoters Stanley Illsley and Leo McCabe, Stan and Oliver and their wives, Ida and Lucille.

The Irish independent Newspaper met the Laurels and the Hardys in the Gresham Hotel. The interview in the May 31st edition read as follows,

"Talking to Mrs. Oliver Hardy and Mrs. Stan Laurel is calculated to upset any preconceived ideas about the gilded palaces of Hollywood. These wives of one of the most popular comedy teams of the film world do their own shopping and their own cooking and cleaning. The husbands help. Mrs. Hardy is a Texan who was brought up in Arizona where her father, a Banker, bought a ranch. She trained as a professional dancer but at eighteen injured her spine and had to give up her dancing career. She took up secretarial work and came to California where she got a job as secretary to writers in the studios.

She graduated to continuity work and then to writing scripts. It was while working on a Laurel and Hardy film that she met her husband.

Mrs. Laurel is a Russian born in Serbia. Her family moved to Harbin in Manchuria, a cosmopolitan city that has been likened to Paris. She learned singing from an Italian maestro. In 1935 she went to the United States, sang a little in opera, gave concerts and secured engagements in nightclubs. One of her brothers had preceded her to America. Four other brothers and a sister, a doctor, remained in Harbin. She has had no word of them or of her mother since before the war and does not know if they are still alive.

The Hardys have moved house recently. Their former home with its large garden was too big. During the war they had grown all their own vegetables there, had kept chickens and even bought a few pigs. But the pigs became such pets that they came running as soon as any of the family opened the back door bowling them over with their enthusiastic welcome. The new house has only two bedrooms.

The Laurels have a seven bedroomed house. Swimming pools are more an incubus than an ornament, they tell me. They cost thirty dollars a month in maintenance, not so much perhaps if they are in use all the time. But the team has been on the move practically since the beginning of the war and their wives have nearly always gone with them.

Longest trip was to France last year when a ten weeks stay on the Riviera proved to Mrs. Hardy and Mrs. Laurel that even sunshine and colour can become oppressive in over-doses.

It is really on those working journeys that the Hardys and the Laurels who seem to be complimentary of each other, are very much together. At home in Hollywood they have each their own circle of friends and find it more stimulating both for their work and their leisure.

But both are what we might call "kitchen" folk. They have a dining nook off the kitchen. Mrs. Hardy told me that even in their bigger house they only used the formal dining room when her family came for Thanksgiving or Christmas dinners. Her mother lives near her. Her sister Betty is not far away either. Before her marriages Betty did film work and was stand-in for Ingrid Bergman. She also modelled for glossy magazines. One brother still lives in Arizona on the family ranch. Constant visitors to the Hardy home are Mr. and Mrs. Pat O'Brien.

Taking a leaf out of her grandmother's book, Mrs. Hardy keeps her larder well stocked. She bottles all the fruit that she grows in her garden and Oliver or "Babe" as his friends call him, is a willing and expert assistant. She discovered that her electric dish-washing machine makes an excellent steriliser for the preserving bottles. Mrs. Laurel's forte is Russian cooking from the traditional Bortsch, a soup made with vegetables including cabbage and served with a blob of sour cream to such mouth-watering delicacies as cotelettes a la Kiev. The latter are made from the slices of the breast of chicken rolled with butter inside and fried. They are served with mushroom sauce. One must be careful when eating them, I understand or the butter may squirt out all over the diner.

The Hardys plan to use a free week which they have after their Belfast engagement to come south again and see more of Ireland. The only difficulty is that neither Laurel nor Hardy can do much in the way of disguise and their appearance in public generally tends to stop the traffic and cause little short of a riot. In Italy they had to step out at half-hour intervals on the balcony of their hotel and wave to waiting fans.

Neither Mrs. Laurel nor Mrs. Hardy can get in much shopping when they travel. Their luggage is already well over weighted. But both are determined to secure some Irish linen. They also talked of Irish crochet gloves as a souvenir of "friendly Ireland". I. M.

Mrs. O. Hardy and Mrs. S. Laurel, wives of the famous comedians.

www.irishnewspaperarchives.com

On June 2nd Stan wrote to Trixie Wyatt on Gresham Hotel headed paper,

We are having a nice time here. Show going well & Bus. good. This is our 2nd week here – then we open at the Opera House Belfast June 19th (2 weeks) well Dear all for now.

Mrs. Laurel joins in kindest regards & every good wish & trust alls well and happy with you. Bye & God bless,

Stan Laurel.

Jammet's Restaurant on Dublin's Nassau Street occupied a pleasant Victorian building and was very much alone in 1952 in offering fine French dining, excellent wines and unparalleled service. Well known as a haunt for well-heeled locals and visiting dignitaries through to the 1960s, John Lennon dined there and as he left remarked, "The other three are saving up to come here". If Oliver Hardy felt that Dublin's hotel prices were expensive, he was to get quite a shock when the Boys dined at Jammet's on one particular evening. They were there at the invitation of the restaurant's owner Louis Jammet who was also a director of the Gate Theatre and as such entertained most of the city's "theatre folk".

Above, the interior of Jammet's Restaurant. Courtesy of TU Dublin

Founded in 1900 on St. Andrew's Street by Louis' father Michel, it was described in a Dublin City directory as a "high class French restaurant".

The restaurant relocated in 1926 to Nassau Street where the centrepiece of their fine new marble and gilt dining rooms, with tables dressed in crisp white linen and the finest crystal glasses flowing with good French Claret, was a mural of the four seasons by the artist Bossini.

When Michel retired in 1928 his son Louis took over. The same year Vogue Magazine described Jammet's as one of Europe's finest restaurants saying it was crowded with gourmets and wits. W.B Yeats had his own table.

Above, the exterior of Jammet's Restaurant. Courtesy of TU Dublin

With his personality and love of theatre, Louis turned Jammet's into an experience more than a restaurant. His personal friends Michael MacLiammor, one of the most recognisable figures in the arts in twentieth century Ireland and Hilton Edwards, known as the founder of Irish theatre, dined there regularly. On many occasions they enjoyed the atmosphere and patronage of the founder of the Gate Theatre, Lord Longford who invariably picked up the bill. They enjoyed it so much they invited Louis to become a director of the Gate Theatre.

Louis continued to run the restaurant through the 1950s and 60s, where, just inside the door was a table known as the Royal Box. Visiting stars from the Theatre Royal would often hold court there and over the years it was frequented by Peter Ustinov, Richard Harris, Josef Locke and Peter O'Toole. The restaurant's guest book reads like a who's who of Hollywood with entries from Walt Disney, Paulette Goddard, Bing Crosby, Elizabeth Taylor, Vivien Leigh and Rita Hayworth.

On one particular evening in June 1952, Stan Laurel and Oliver Hardy accepted an invitation to dine there. During the conversation Stan mentioned his love of fishing and the tagged perch he had heard so much about in Poulaphouca Lake in County Wicklow. With theatrical circles being what they are, it was suggested that a visit could be organised to include lunch in the Glen Heste Hotel, which had links to Dublin's theatre world. Oliver Hardy we know was fond of putting in his day by taking a car journey out of the city and going sightseeing around the countryside and had taken numerous journeys like this on this tour already. He had taken in many tourist sites around England and Scotland. County Wicklow was close enough to Dublin to enable such a day trip.

Known as the Garden of Ireland because of its unspoilt, breath-taking landscape, it must have been quite tempting to the visitors. And so, the two men along with their wives, set off early one morning for the hour long car journey out of Dublin, to County Wicklow and to the Poulaphouca Reservoir. The reservoir was created between 1937 and 1947, with flooding beginning in at 10 am on 3 March 1940 by damming Dublin's River Liffey at Poulaphouca as part of the Electricity Supply Board project to build a second hydroelectric station in Ireland. As is usual when new land flooding occurs, the river fish grew to unprecedented sizes and in number due to the rich land feeding. Trout grew hugely and some reported catches of up to 4 and 5lbs were common. Perch grew to such extreme numbers that in the late 1950s, the Irish government Department of Fisheries had to intervene and introduce controlled netting and trapping in an effort to reduce their population.

With such an interest in fishing Stan must have thoroughly enjoyed his time in this most scenic of surroundings, however it is not known if he actually got the chance to fish or not. The party made their way to the local village of Manor Kilbride where they lunched at the Glen Heste Hotel, which was no ordinary rural hotel. Part owned by Harry O'Donovan, a script writer for famous Irish actors, Maureen Potter and Jimmy O'Dea, Harry was known to have welcomed many famous faces over the years from the world of theatre and film to the hotel.

The community of Manor Kilbride were quite proud, having such an elite hotel in their village that catered to the more elite and attracted a certain clientele. With horse riding, shooting and fishing on offer in the plush surroundings, there was enough land on its ninety acres to incorporate lavish gardens within the secluded surrounds of the Glen Heste Hotel. More importantly however, it had its own private airfield situated at the rear of the building which attracted a lot of affluent guests arriving at Shannon airport. This alone was extremely appealing to some Hollywood stars who wanted to avoid the enthusiastic fandom that celebrity status brought and could simply fly on to a secluded hotel in the middle of the Irish countryside.

The Boys and their wives enjoyed the company of Harry who made much of the fact that he had the two most famous comedians in the world at his hotel. Word had mysteriously leaked out to the small village community that Laurel and Hardy were at the hotel and a stream of young and old admirers began arriving and vying for the best viewing positions outside the building. Of course Stan and Oliver were not going to allow anyone to miss out and they signed each and every piece of paper and spoke to all the children.

They spent so much time enjoying the hospitality of Manor Kilbride and Harry O'Donovan that Stan became a little worried about the trip back and their curtain time at the Olympia for that night's show. The story was, that their driver had to break the occasional speed limit in order to get them back to the city in time.

The hotel itself was destroyed by fire in suspicious circumstances in 1958. Three years beforehand, Mr. Maynard Boyd, the hotel's owner at the time had mysteriously disappeared, causing a nationwide search. He turned up days later in York, England citing memory loss. After the fire the insurance claim was halted by a Dublin judge who had issue with the rebuilding cost being quoted at £8000 when in fact a prominent building firm had estimated £30,000. The claim was settled out of court and the hotel was never rebuilt.

Even today, an air of mystery surrounds the events of 1958. During research for this publication a visit was taken to Manor Kilbride to view the site of the hotel and our experiences there were nothing short of a Scooby Doo script. Whilst not being warned off completely, we were told in no uncertain terms, "Oh you don't want to visit there. You'd do well to avoid that place." We found ourselves with no information forthcoming regarding the location of the ruined building. After much searching we did eventually find the site of the hotel and the last remaining structure. Now overgrown with ivy and hidden off road on the grounds of a private dwelling, the ruins of the hotel became just that, slowly disappearing over the years.

Above, the Glen Heste Hotel during the early 1940s and left, the entrance archway, all that remains today.

The Support Acts

Laurel and Hardy played to a packed house twice a night plus matinees twice weekly, for two weeks at the Olympia. They topped the bill that consisted of a host of performers who had been accompanying them on their current tour.

The supporting artists who accompanied Stan and Oliver on their tour were exactly what you might call variety. And this is precisely what the show was all about. Their life on the road may not have been as comfortable as Stan and Oliver's with hotel stays not really an option. Instead, cheaper lodging houses and digs would have been their arrangement, and the cost would have to have been covered by themselves. The Boys became quite close with all the acts as you would expect and they remained in contact with some of them for many years.

The Lonsdale Sisters performed a mixture of synchronised modern dance and tap dance and were comprised of Pauline Cingalee and Florence Samuels. Pauline was slightly younger and met Florence when the two girls were on tour with their families. Pauline was the daughter of The Great Cingalee and she taught Florence how to dance. Her father suggested they take it to the stage as an act and the Lonsdale Sisters were born. Although not blood related Florence did marry Pauline's uncle who was working with them as a stage hand and thus made them niece and aunt. After the tour of 1952 Stan and Oliver remained in close contact with the sisters via letters and by constantly reading variety papers to follow their careers.

Jimmie Elliot was an animal mimic whose stage act involved him coming on stage as though he was just coming in from a day's hunting. Dressed in African safari attire he proceeded to take the audience through a day at the farm with squabbling pigs and disobedient dogs, right up to arrogant cattle and hungry chickens and then ending his act with a dog fight. A bizarre act by today's standards but you can see the fun and attraction that the act might have had when you think that Steve Irwin did something similar by bringing his audience into an animal world many years later on television. Jimmie worked for BBC radio and used this as an attraction to get stage work but it is not sure in what capacity he actually worked for the broadcaster. Some years after he appeared with the Boys on stage it looks like he retired. A letter from Stan, sent to Lawrence Lorraine in 1955 stated,

```
"Was pleased to note Jimmy Elliot has a nice steady
job, he's certainly better off, am sure he will be
much happier".
```

Jimmie (Jimmy) Elliot

Archie Elray, sometimes billed as "The Family Ventriloquist", or "The Vitamin Ventriloquist" was a hugely popular music hall act who appeared on a host of playbills up and down the U.K. between the 1940s and 1960s. He used three life sized dummies and was sometimes assisted in his act by Dorothy who was written as Dorothy Elray in one review, showing that it was his wife. When Dorothy was not with him he was billed as "Archie Elray and Co". A review of his act on September 13th 1948 states,

"Archie Elray assisted by Dorothy Elray was second on the bill and earned a big mitt with his ventriloquist act. He used three dummies moved thru (sic) a control box from behind one of the dummies." This was quite ingenious and must have been pretty amazing and probably very funny.

Archie, 3rd from left! With Dorothy at the back and the three connected dummies. Courtesy of Roger Robinson

Mackenzie Reid and Dorothy were a husband and wife team consisting of John Reid and Dorothy MacKenzie, who were described as "Ace Accordionists". Also billed as Scotland's Accordionists they arrived on stage wearing kilts and very quickly had the theatre clapping and tapping their feet. They had accompanied Laurel and Hardy for much of their 1947 tour and they were on almost every bill for the 1952 tour. In November 1953 they were the second act on stage at the Royal Variety performance in London in front of the new Queen, Elizabeth, her husband Prince Philip and sister Princess Margaret. Sadly, two months later, John passed away. He was quite ill at the time that they had appeared in front of the Queen. Dorothy continued performing with a new partner and was billed as "Dorothy Reid and Mack". They joined the 1954 Laurel and Hardy tour and remained a part of that until the final date in Plymouth meaning that she was the only act that supported Laurel and Hardy on all of their tours of Britain and Ireland.

MacKenzie Reid and Dorothy. Photo by Frank Darlington, courtesy of Edinburghcollected.org

Lorraine, the Singing Cartoonist is an interesting act. Intensive research unearthed absolutely nothing about her and I am indebted to the sleuthing skills of Roger Robinson for solving the mystery of her name and his conclusions about her act. She was in fact a he! Correspondence between Stan Laurel and Lorraine showed that her real name was in fact Lawrence Lorraine, a man. Sometimes billed as Lorraine and partner, who was in fact, his wife Jeanette. The conclusion is, that Lorraine called certain members of the audience onstage and drew their caricatures whilst singing to them. Charming in its own way but possibly difficult to follow from the seats at the back. Lawrence sent Stan a personal painting which he thanked him for and said **"it will hang in the living room and remain a happy memory of our tour with you."**

The Great Cingalee, "The Silent Man of Mystery in Wonders of the East" in the company of "Skilled Mystifiers", is sometimes how this interesting act was billed. A mysterious illusionist is another description of this strange performance. Coming from a family of performers, his father was also a "Mystifier", with the London Standard newspaper describing him as such in a piece from March 2nd 1905. Born Claude Albert Francis Banks in 1900 he, along with his wife Marie who was one of his assistants during his act, and daughter Pauline of the Lonsdale Sisters, struck up something of a friendship with Stan and Oliver. A friendship that lasted long after the tour ended. Performing on the stage from a young age, he had even acted in a long lost British film called "Can You Hear Me Mother?" as a conjurer.

A photograph from his granddaughter Shelli's collection has an inscription from Oliver Hardy where he calls himself the "non-drinker". Knowing that Oliver Hardy liked a drink, we assume that he and Claude were drinking buddies on occasion. Letters from Lucille Hardy to Claude and Marie show a real fondness and affection for each other's families when both Oliver and Claude were not well and recovering from illness.

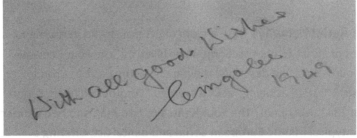

Cingalee above and his autograph below, from the author's collection

Claude "Cingalee" Banks with the Boys. Courtesy of Roger Robinson. From the collection of Claude's granddaughter Shelli, with thanks.

The Aerial Kenways were a team of gymnasts who performed a series of aerial acrobatics. Sometimes billed as "The Four Kenways", Billboard Magazine described their act from the Casino in London on August 9th 1948 as being "above average." Another Billboard report from 1943 described, **"The Four Kenways, two men and two women are a typical middle European aerial and dental act, offering a miscellany of good but not striking stunts and win appreciation."** More than likely of circus origin and a family act but sadly little more is known about them.

Dubliner George Boyle, was taken by his father to see one of the shows in the Olympia and described its opening to me as follows,

"We were sitting in our seats and knew from the programme that Laurel and Hardy were the next act on. We had enjoyed the show but this was what we had come to see. There seemed to be a long delay between the last act and Laurel and Hardy and the curtains stayed closed. Maybe it was supposed to be like that but after what seemed like a long time the curtains were still closed. Then someone at the back of the theatre began to laugh. It started as a bit of a giggle but then someone else began laughing. It caused more people to start laughing and pretty soon, the whole theatre was laughing like crazy and they still hadn't come out yet! When they did finally emerge, they were greeted by a house full of laughing people and I mean really laughing. It must have been wonderful for them."

In a small bar at the back of the theatre a young barmaid named Maureen Grant was busily going about her duties. She knew who Laurel and Hardy were and obviously knew that they were the main act. When she heard the house laughing so much on the opening night, she ran out of the bar and took a peek at just what it was that was so very funny. Before she had realised, the act was over and she had been away from her duties for almost thirty minutes. Thankfully the fact that it was Laurel and Hardy onstage meant that everyone was watching the show and strangely enough for an Irish bar, nobody had been looking for a drink!

Over the next two weeks she had the pleasure of serving drinks to Stan and Oliver and their wives after the shows.

"They used to come in and sit on the long bench seat that ran along the wall. It was close to the heater so it was the warmest spot to be. There was a huge Aspidistra plant sitting on the counter and Stan often messed around with it, pretending to hide in its large leaves. They were lovely and we had two wonderful weeks with them. Their wives were real ladies and their fur coats made me quite envious. They had no airs and graces and were some of the nicest people we've ever had at the theatre."

Maureen had only just begun working at the theatre. She retired aged ninety in 2017. The bar she worked in for so long is now named "Maureen's Bar". She is quite a character and loved to recount all the famous people who performed at the Olympia over the years. She worked all her life and even hid her pregnancies from her employers, taking holiday leave when each baby was due to be born. They believed her to be childless.

In 1974 part of the roof above the stage collapsed and the theatre was closed. It remained closed for two and a half years and began to fall into disrepair. Maureen was instrumental in getting it opened again. She campaigned as part of a team that tried to get Dublin Corporation and the backing of famous people to get the theatre opened again. On one occasion she could be seen on the back of a low loader truck that was driven up and down O'Connell Street, shaking buckets and looking for donations. When the Sons of the Desert European Convention was hosted in Dublin in 2007, Maureen welcomed us all into the theatre allowing us access to the stage where Laurel and Hardy had performed all those years before.

Maureen Grant on the occasion of the 2007 European Convention wearing a Sons of the Desert fez that was presented to her.

Dublin resident Patrick O'Leary had a very interesting pastime. He loved the theatre. Every spare moment he had would see him to visit one of Dublin's many playhouses and take in a show. Some Saturdays would see Patrick seeing a morning show in the Theatre Royal then perhaps a matinee in the Gate Theatre and onto an evening performance in the Olympia. He lost count of the amount of shows he must have seen but does remember one act very clearly and it holds a special place in his heart. The night he saw Laurel and Hardy.

"I must have seen thousands of shows. Any chance I had to go to the theatre and then the pictures, I took it. I went alone. I didn't mind though because I felt like I was friends with all the performers. It felt like they were performing just for me. Watching Laurel and Hardy felt the same. They were great. I remember laughing so much at their antics. Everyone in the theatre was really enjoying it. It felt like we were all one big family that night because you could feel the warmth from them. I never felt that atmosphere at any other time."

Stan and Oliver were seen out and about on the streets of Dublin.

"I saw them on Henry Street once. I can't remember if they were alone or not but they were both there. It was not what you could call a mob scene but with lots of people surrounding them and asking for autographs it must have been very time consuming for them if they were on a shopping trip. Some people did not believe it was actually Laurel and Hardy and just kept walking on. Imagine missing out on a chance like that? N.W.

On another occasion they were spotted leaving the Gresham Hotel and walking up O'Connell Street as if to take a stroll. People walked past the famous duo and did double takes, not believing that they could have possibly walked past Laurel and Hardy. As soon as one person stopped to talk to them and ask for an autograph a crowd developed and after a while they simply returned to the hotel unable to continue their walk.

Oliver Hardy was known to be a lobby watcher. He would spend a lot of time just sitting in a comfortable armchair in a hotel lobby and simply watching everyone going about their business. He was doing this one day in an armchair which was situated just inside the main door of the Gresham Hotel. A young lady walked past and thought she saw Oliver Hardy sitting there. She paused and retraced her steps. She could not believe it was actually him. Normally shy and lacking confidence she knew that she would never have an opportunity to meet a Hollywood star like this again. She summoned up all her courage and walked inside and stood in front of Mr. Hardy and offered her hand. He smiled and shook it and said "hello". Asking for an autograph, Oliver asked one of the young porters to get him some writing paper and duly supplied the signature which is reproduced below with thanks. (The lady in question wished to remain anonymous).

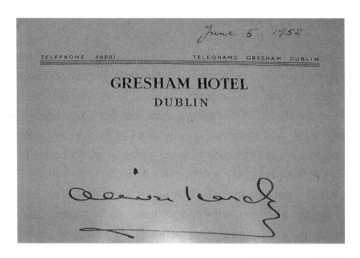

Oliver explained that Stan was resting and unable to sign an autograph for her but did suggest that she call back later, something she regrets not doing. Stan may have been resting or he may possibly have been up in his room attending to his own correspondence as the following postcard, signed to a young fan shows. It is dated with the same date as Oliver Hardy's autograph on hotel paper.

The Boys received a lot of post whilst they were staying in Dublin and Stan tried to answer every single piece.

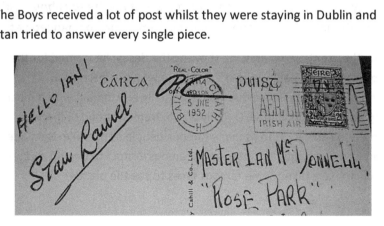

One of these pieces of post was an invitation to see the birthplace of George Bernard Shaw, the famous Irish playwright, critic and political activist. It came from a man named Patrick O'Reilly who had been a dustman in the area of Dublin where Shaw was born. Correspondence between O'Reilly and Shaw was intense and the two became friends. Patrick made it his life's mission to erect a plaque on the house in Synge Street where Shaw was born and began a collection, not only of Dublin dustbin rubbish but also from the owners of those dustbins. Years later he had collected enough money and sold enough 'rag and bone' to erect the plaque and asked Shaw if he liked the wording and would Shaw approve the inscription,

"He gave his services to his country, unlimited, unstinted and without price."

Shaw's reply was typical.

"Dear Pat: Your inscription is a blazing lie. I left Dublin before I was twenty and I have devoted the remainder of my life to Labour and International Socialism and for all you know I may be hanged yet."

Shaw then sent over a drawing showing the design he wanted for the plaque – a wreath of shamrocks in marble with the inscription mentioned above. The plaque was eventually erected but with a much simpler inscription. Patrick O'Reilly was extremely proud of it and wanted to show it off to as many famous people as possible. He made a point of trying to get in contact with famous visitors to Ireland and was known to have taken some famous faces to see the plaque.

He wrote to Laurel and Hardy at the Olympia and left a photograph for them. Stan wrote the reply on Gresham Hotel headed paper and signed it Laurel and Hardy.

"Dear Mr. O'Reilly, Thank you for the photograph you left at the theatre. We asked for you to come up and see us but you didn't show up. We would have liked to have seen the birthplace of your old friend the late Bernard Shaw but we have so much to do in relation to our business, we don't have the time to do many things we would like to. However we are hoping to return here on a vacation – then we can go places and enjoy everything. Again thanks, regards and every good wishes. Sincerely always Laurel & Hardy."

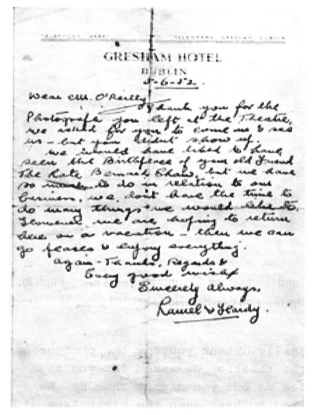

The letter that Stan wrote to Patrick O'Reilly regretfully declining an invitation to see the birthplace of George Bernard Shaw. The letter came up for auction in a Dublin auction house in 2015 and was sold in a framed display for €520.

Earl Connolly was Entertainments Reporter for The Limerick Leader newspaper for over half a century. He lunched with Charlton Heston in London just before the premiere of The Ten Commandments.

Danny Kaye, Jimmy Durante and Ingrid Bergman were counted amongst his many friends and those who knew him smiled at the mention of his very name, he was so well thought of. In his spare time, if you could call it that, he managed and was part of a showband called The Sylvian who travelled thousands of miles all over Ireland as they played in what were known as "The Ballrooms of Romance" during the hugely popular showband era of the 1950s and 60s.

His love of cinema was behind his trip to Dublin to meet two great comedians who he had followed from an early age and had a great affection for. The following photographs were taken backstage at the Olympia Theatre and are reproduced courtesy of his wife Callie. The first shows Earl with the Boys.

The above picture has, from left to right, Callie Connolly, Earl Connolly, Stan, Jim Marshall, Jim O'Carroll, Mrs. Murphy, Oliver and Ida Laurel.

Earl's article for the Limerick Leader stated,

"Last Friday night I fulfilled a lifelong ambition when I met the comedy kings in person. In appearance Stan is exactly as you have seen him in the countless films. There the resemblance ends. He greets you in a deep cultured voice, friendly to the extreme and at once endears himself as one who loves to meet his public. When I ask him about their future plans he said that "next year we hope to go into television and make some films specially for that medium."

Just then his 22 stone partner came along. Oliver is stouter in person than on the screen but his big warm smile is something that audiences would love to see for themselves. He is a joyful person who speaks with a pronounced American accent. Describing Stanley as "my right arm" it was obvious that they are the happiest pair on earth. To my question: "What do you think of Irish audiences"? he bounced back with the question. "What do Irish audiences think of us?" My answer was an emphatic, "You are still top favourites in this country. This pleased the pair.

Seeing them together convinces one that this lovable pair are happy in the knowledge that they have made the world laugh. They make you feel that they have been your friend for years, and a half an hour slipped by as we discussed films and audiences. All that time they were most helpful and cooperative.

Their Stage Act

Their stage act incorporates most of the routines that you have seen them do on the screen, all instantly recognisable. To see them in person was a rare privilege and on behalf of their legion of fans here may I thank them most sincerely for so generously giving me so much of their valuable time in order to make this story possible. Thank you Ollie and Stan."

Earl's article continued with a very surprising addition. One that I have never been aware of. I have made numerous attempts to locate the subject of it, to no avail. I pledge to keep looking.

LAUREL AND HARDY SEND GREETINGS TO AUDIENCES.

During the course of this exclusive interview with Laurel and Hardy (the only one granted to a provincial film correspondent, I understand) they also made a recording (on tape) for Mr. J. A. O'Carroll.

This greeting extends their regards to the rural audiences on Mr. O'Carroll's Movie Circuit in Counties Limerick and Tipperary. It will be played to them this week prior to the screening of the main feature. Stan asked to hear the complete recording (which included a special introduction by Mr. O'Carroll) and the two comedians expressed keen interest in the apparatus used and praised the high quality of the sound. Coming from men who have heard "play-backs" of "sound tracks" of their voices on Hollywood's most expensive equipment, this was praise indeed.

The comedy kings posed for several pictures with individual members of our party and altogether made the occasion a memorable and pleasant one."

Exciting indeed to think that there may be an unknown recording of Laurel and Hardy somewhere. Hope indeed that one day the missing films "The Rogue Song" and "Hats Off" may be found.

****

Earl's wife Callie couldn't say nicer things about Stan and Oliver when we spoke by phone in 2019. Sadly Earl had died some years before but she was so intent on making sure that she shared all his adventures and encounters with so many famous and wonderful people that she was only too pleased to be a part of this publication. She recounted that

Mrs. Laurel was so friendly and kind to her that all these years later the impact that she felt from Stan's wife was still with her.

"Such a lady and they were easily the nicest gentlemen I have ever come across. I can't say enough about them I really can't. We invited them to lunch and this happened the very next day. I remember it was in a hotel nearer the river Liffey than their hotel. Not the Cleary's side, the other side. The name escapes me but the memory doesn't. Such gentlemen and such lovely ladies."

(The hotel was most likely The Metropole which was beside the GPO and is sadly now gone).

Another provincial newspaper, The Munster Express reported the following,

"Laurel and Hardy In The Flesh"

"This week whilst our Editor was staying in the Gresham Hotel in Dublin, he met the film star comedians Laurel and Hardy who are also staying at that hotel with their wives. He has been thoughtful enough to pass me the following "close up" of the homely pair.

Who was in their company most of the time was a nun, Sister Camelia of the order of Our Divine Saviour. They had never met before until, fortuitously on the "Queen Mary" during the Atlantic journey across.

Laurel and Hardy are a big success at the Olympia Theatre in Dublin last week and are also booked for Belfast for the following two weeks. Hardy is the stouter one of the comedians and the most serious of the pair. Laurel is always inclined to be light in humour and ready for a joke. Both were dressed in light summer clothes, but Laurel wore a blue beret, even in the hotel, whilst Hardy wore glasses. Both are not ageing too much but were taking things easy. Not exactly tee-totallers they rarely over-do anything, conserving their energy for their stage audiences. Laurel married early in life and now has a daughter married with a family of her own, making him a grandfather. Hardy is not, however, blessed with a family but his wife is most charming and of pre-possessing appearance.

They are delighted with their visit to Ireland and particularly with the public and private welcomes they are receiving, in fact the Cead Mile Failtes that are extended to them privately are particularly appreciated, and they aver that Ireland is unique in that, the people but maintaining its reputation of "Ireland of the Welcomes."

Lest it might be assumed that these famous comedians being in the company of a nun, are Catholics, such is not the case. It must be said that they are impressed with the religious fervour of the Irish.

It was fascinating to see big Hardy in the flesh and he is just as fleshy as on the screen, weighing about 22 stones. They attracted as much attention at the hotel and the staff there declared they were a pleasure to entertain."

Sunday Independent May 25th

www.irishnewspaperarchives.com

By all accounts, the time that Stan and Oliver spent in Dublin in 1952 was extremely happy and joyful, not only for the two men themselves but for each and every Irish person who met or saw them onstage. Their kind nature in giving up so much of their time to meet and greet people and tell their story and answer each and every questions is testament to how much they appreciated the public who had enjoyed their films so much and who now came to simply see them in person and tell these two men how much they loved them.

From speaking to those who met and saw them perform, I can only conclude that such lasting, happy memories come from a love of two amazing human beings who did not disappoint. Memories that last to this day, almost seventy years later. Memories that still get resurrected at family get-togethers and stories that are forever being begged to be retold again and again.

Fifty three years later in October 2005, Laurel and Hardy appeared once more onstage at the Olympia Theatre in the form of Tom McGrath's play, "Laurel and Hardy" as part of the Dublin Theatre Festival. This time Steven McNicoll and Barnaby Power had the huge job of playing the Boys and this they did with perfect accuracy under the direction of Tony Cownie and the musical accompaniment of Jon Beales.

A contingent from the Irish Sons of the Desert decided to make a night of it and quite by accident found themselves sitting rather close to the stage one night, adorned in Laurel and Hardy t-shirts and fezzes. I can only imagine what might have been going through the actor's heads as they walked onstage in their best Stan and Ollie mode which they had probably rehearsed to exactness, then catching a glimpse of a large number of Laurel and Hardy fanatics who would be criticising their every move. Not so. We were there to enjoy the antics of a live version of the Boys and they were fantastic in their portrayal. Even if they had not been as accurate as they were, we would have applauded.

The photo below was taken in the green room at the theatre which is the exact same room that the photos with Earl Connolly were taken all those years ago with Stan and Oliver and include the author.

Left, Steven McNicoll and Barnaby Power as Laurel and Hardy in Tom McGrath's play.

The following advertisements appeared in Dublin's newspapers in 1952.

"We're well up in the queue now, Ollie!"

www.irishnewspaperarchives.com

Stan and Oliver played their last show in Dublin on 7th June. The next day they said their goodbyes to the staff of the Gresham Hotel who were sorry to be losing their famous guests. They had grown fond of these two giants of the screen and would miss them both very much. Mary O'Brien worked as a maid at the hotel and remembered the perfectly mannered gentlemen that were Laurel and Hardy. "Staff members used to argue over who would clean their room or take them tea and biscuits. Sometimes it wasn't just to get a chance to meet them, it was the chance to get a good tip. They weren't like some of the guests we used to get, they tipped really well and word got around very quickly about that and it caused good natured arguments amongst the staff. Mrs. Laurel and Mrs. Hardy were so nice to us. They talked to us like we were their friends and not there staff. Mrs. Laurel was like a film star herself. She looked fabulous all the time, even first thing in the morning! But she always asked how I was and how my family were."

The touring party took the Enterprise train from Dublin's Connolly station to Belfast. Tom Laidlaw was a twelve year old train spotter. He was at the station when he noticed a small bit of commotion behind him. As he turned he noticed two photographers laughing out loud at the antics of another two men and not realising what was going on, he then heard someone say that it was Laurel and Hardy. He remembers the two men having to haul a couple of very large trunks behind them as they made their way all the way down to carriage five or six. Oliver Hardy led the way and was followed by Stan and the two ladies.

The two photographers continued taking photographs as he himself stared open mouthed not believing what was taking place in front of him. To this day he still can't understand why nobody helped with the trunks choosing instead to laugh and smile at the entire scenario. **"Oliver twiddled his tie and waved his little wave as he sweated with the weight of the trunks. Everyone thought they were putting on an act for us but afterwards I realised that they were just trying to get on a train with a couple of heavy trunks!"**

Belfast

Having spent a thoroughly enjoyable time in Dublin the touring party took the train to Belfast in time to open on June 9th. Two weeks were booked and they were playing two shows per night at the Grand Opera House with a matinee on Saturdays. If they thought the people of Dublin loved Laurel and Hardy they were about to quickly find out that the people of Belfast probably loved them even more, as an article in the Belfast Telegraph was titled as follows,

"Laurel and Hardy are Prisoners in Belfast".

The Boys were staying at the Midland Hotel in Whitla Street also known as the Midland Station Hotel due to being situated right beside the railway station which was very convenient for Messer's Laurel and Hardy. This grand hotel was opened in 1898 and built in the Victorian style of the period. It was operated by the Belfast and Northern Counties Railway Company who were vying for business from weary tourists disembarking from the railway station directly beside the hotel. The railway terminus at the Midland was in fact attached to the building itself. Competing railway companies were building hotels all across the province in an effort to boost business. The clientele would have been commercial and tourist in nature and more than likely from the upper classes and as there were no other hotels in that area, the Midland would have gained the business. The hotel was destroyed in the Blitz of Belfast in Easter 1941, along with much of the original railway terminus.

It was rebuilt and thrived in what later became an isolated part of Belfast until the 1980s when it was converted to use as offices by the Hastings Hotel Group. The building was demolished in 2017.

The Midland Hotel at roughly the time the Boys stayed there.

The Telegraph was referring to the fact that Stan and Oliver couldn't leave their hotel rooms for the majority of their stay except to go to the Opera House to work. Mob scenes accompanied them whenever they left their room. They desperately wanted to see some of the city but the only sightseeing that could be done was from a car. Even eating at the hotel restaurant was impossible and food had to be taken to their rooms. Oliver Hardy spoke to a reporter by telephone and said, **"We've had a wonderful reception in Belfast, and we'd hate it too if we weren't recognised. But as things are, we just have to stay locked up in here."**

```
        GRAND
   OPERA HOUSE
   Next Week 6.40 and 8.55 (Saturday
   6 and 8.15). Matinee Saturday 2.30.
   LAUREL AND HARDY
        Reserved 2/6, 3/-, 4/6, 5/-;
              Unreserved 1/6.
   Children Half-price First House and
                 Matinee.
```

Hotel staff described them as delightful and very lovely men. Children and adults alike would line up at the Opera House stage door each night and when the taxi arrived carrying the famous comedians, they got out and spoke to everyone. They smiled and waved and were described by all as being "just lovely." One person described Oliver Hardy being helped out of the car as he struggled to exit the vehicle alone.

Occasionally they came out onto their hotel balcony and waved at the crowds below to huge applause. "We simply wanted to see them and for them to know we were there for them", said one eyewitness.

103

Each night they were hurriedly ushered through the hotel lobby and into a waiting car before being taken to the theatre. One afternoon a young man was walking past the hotel on his way home and could not believe it when out of the door stepped Laurel and Hardy.
"I walked over and said "Good afternoon Mr. Hardy, Good afternoon Mr. Laurel Thank you for all the happiness." They held out their hands to shake mine and Ollie pushed Stan's hand away as he had probably done many times before. Then they got into the car and drove off. I thought I had dreamt it all. I can still see their faces and I will never forget that moment." The man was Frank Carson who years later became a famous Irish comedian and a staple on British television during the 1970s and 80s.

Frank Carson, Irish Comedian 1926-2012

The Grand Opera House in Belfast held its first performance on 23rd December 1895 and has been hosting some of the biggest names in show business ever since. Gracie Fields made an appearance in 1933 to sell out audiences. Dwight Eisenhower arrived one evening in 1945 in the company of Field Marshall Montgomery and they were treated to a show by the Savoy Players, a company of actors who were famous in Ireland at the time.

In 1963 an unknown singer named Luciano Pavarotti made his stage debut at the Opera House in Madame Butterfly.

By the 1970s, civil unrest in the city caused problems for the theatre with night time audiences virtually disappearing. Despite all efforts to keep it as a working theatre it was eventually sold to property developers who planned to demolish it and redevelop the site.

The Ulster Architectural Society became interested and undertook a campaign to try to save the building from demolition and in 1974 the Grand Opera House was given the distinction of being the first building in Northern Ireland to become listed. The future still was not certain however as the building was not in a state fit for theatrical use and needed extensive renovation. Thankfully the Arts Council became involved, bought it back from the developers and took on the job of restoring the building to a working theatre once more.

Between 1976 and 1980, major works were carried out with emphasis on retaining as much of the original features as possible including the ornate ceiling panels in the main auditorium.

It survived two car bombs during the 1990s and blast walls were built to protect it from future damage. Today it is operated by the Grand Opera House Trust and has had major extension and renovation works adding additional dressing rooms and hospitality areas including lifts between floors.

The Grand Opera House in Belfast advertising Laurel and Hardy onstage, with queues forming for the evening's show. Courtesy of "Old Belfast Facebook"

Johnny Murphy worked at the Opera House in the 1950s and one night he noticed that the Boys, having just left the theatre had forgotten to take a fur coat from their dressing room. Johnny ran out after them and they were so pleased that he was rewarded with ten shillings tip!

Ann Tome was a fourteen year old girl at the time and desperately wanted to see her heroes on stage in her home town. Tickets were like gold dust and the shows were completely sold out. Not one to be put off, she wrote to Stan at the hotel and duly received a telegram from him inviting her to come to the show the very next day.

A rare photo taken onstage in Belfast on Monday 16th June celebrating Stan's birthday. Laurel and Hardy and the supporting acts. From the collection of Andreas Baum with thanks.

Jim Hanna worked as a Barber in Belfast, not too far from the Midland Hotel. Sometimes the shop would receive a phone call from the reception at the hotel asking for a barber to come and give a haircut to one of the guests. One particular day, the phone rang and was answered. The hotel explained that it was Laurel and Hardy who needed haircuts and could someone come around.

Jim remembers being asked to go and initially he refused saying that he would be too scared to cut the hair of such giants of the screen. However he soon composed himself and made his way to the hotel which had a room set aside especially for such visits. Jim went to the room but was told that due to the mob scenes outside, he would have to go up to the guest's suites.

Jim took the stairs to Oliver Hardy's suite with his legs trembling and knocked on the door which was opened by Mrs. Hardy who invited him in. Jim asked Oliver how he would like his hair cut and Oliver replied, "Just a trim." Jim remembers the chair was too small to accommodate Hardy's bulk and so he simply perched on the edge of it. There wasn't a lot of talk between the two men, just pleasantries. When Jim finished, Oliver looked in the mirror and said, "Jolly good", before taking the telephone and calling ahead to Stan. "Stanley, the barber's here." Jim remembered feeling like an executioner when he heard that. Oliver then paid Jim his money and gave him a one pound tip

Jim then made to way to Stan's suite which according to Jim, was the top suite. Mrs. Laurel opened the door and he was invited in with a smile. Stan was wearing a smoking jacket and smiled at him. Jim asked Stan how he would like his hair and Stan walked into the bathroom, came out a few moments later with damp hair and said, "I don't want much off, just a little as I have to keep it line with my act." Jim cut a little off Stan's hair and was paid his fee plus another huge one pound tip.

He returned to the barbers shop and gave up the fee that he had been paid and boasted of his two pound tip which he said was his before putting it into his pocket. The owner of the shop Lily Myers was quick to get two printed bowler hat signs for the window with the words, "We cut the hair of Laurel and Hardy. Why not let us cut yours?"

During their stay they were asked to judge a singing contest that was taking place at the Tonic Cinema in Bangor. Because of concerns over their safety and the risk of being mobbed even further they were warned against taking part. Not wanting to let anyone down they agreed to judge the competition when it was suggested that it could be broadcast over the radio and they could listen to it in their dressing room at the Opera House. And that is exactly what they did.

Another great story from Belfast concerns a local upholsterer named Charlie Donaghy. Charlie was known for his fabulous singing voice and was also known to go busking outside the Opera House. One evening a large crowd waiting for the doors to open in order that they could go inside and see Laurel and Hardy onstage, were listening as Charlie entertain them with a rendition of "St. Teresa of the Roses", when a large black car pulled up in front of him. Out stepped Oliver Hardy and Stan Laurel. Oliver walked over to Charlie and the crowd looked on in awe as Oliver, who was subsequently joined by his partner, listened intently until Charlie finished singing. Oliver put his hand in his pocket and handed Charlie a half crown coin.

From then on Charlie told everyone that he was the only person who had the pleasure of singing personally for the world's greatest comedy duo.

Renowned Belfast street fighter "Buck Alec" Robinson was one of the cities famous and more bizarre characters. He was even credited with being a driver for Al Capone. He kept three lions at the back of his house (*yes, you read it correctly, three lions*) and could regularly be seen walking one of them around the streets of Belfast, quite casually. He invited Stan and Oliver to his home to see his lions and they accepted. Buck Alec's wife told everyone the story that she was washing the children in a zinc bath in front of the fire when her husband just walked through the house with Laurel and Hardy in tow!

While in Belfast, Stan celebrated his 62nd birthday. Three cakes were made to celebrate the occasion with the story that one cake would be too small to hold all the candles. It was presented to him backstage at the theatre.

Weeks of touring had taken their toll on Stan and it was agreed that he should take a week off to recuperate. The weeks beginning 23rd and 30th June were listed by Stan, in a letter dated 24th March 1952 to his old friend Booth Coleman, as being "open". This was more than likely left that way in order to give the Boys some free time as they were more or less half way through their tour. Stan checked into the Musgrave and Clark Clinic which was part of the Royal Victoria Hospital. He would spend a week there in order to get some rest. He insisted that a desk be brought into his room so that he could keep up with his correspondence and this was supplied.

While Stan was there he made daily trips into several wards in the hospital, to visit other patients and cheer them up. The nurses who accompanied him on these walkabouts said the Stan was so nice to the other patients and so very understanding and funny that spirits lifted across the entire hospital.

But Stan was taking a hospital stay for a reason. He was tired and very thin. His diabetes had become something of a worry for his doctors and one day Mrs. Laurel phoned to check up on his progress.

The doctor assigned to Stan, Dr. Smith, came on the phone and explained that he was having trouble getting his blood sugars stabilised. Mrs. Laurel made the doctor promise not to tell Stan that she had told him but suggested that he look under Stan's pillow and into his suitcase. This the doctor did, and Stan's sweet tooth was found to be the cause of the trouble. Empty sweet wrappers and even a small box of chocolates were found under his pillow and inside his case. His condition became much better afterwards.

Three of Stan's nurses gave accounts of his time there. All three told exactly the same story of a very nice man whose thoughts were of others. He spent a lot of time at his desk writing letters and asking the nurses to post them for him. He was constantly being funny and carrying on with his mannerisms of scratching his head and pretending to bump into things and getting hurt.

He signed autographs for all members of staff, some of whom kept a constant visitation to the room. Nurse Nancy Jane Reid described him as a gentleman and Nurse Grace Gault explained that he liked to eat his meal late at night usually around 11pm.

Nurse Minnie Raye (sometimes Ray), told the same tales about Stan. She said that one day Oliver Hardy turned up unexpectedly at the hospital to see Stan and the staff were in awe of him and could not believe that now the two comedians were there. Oliver had decided to take a day out from a Dublin holiday and took the train journey north in order to check up on the well-being of his partner, perhaps giving another insight into their close friendship. Apparently the two men spent much of their time laughing and enquiring on the health of the other patients.

As mentioned, while Stan was at the clinic, Mr. and Mrs. Hardy decided to return to Dublin for a week's holiday. They booked into the Shelbourne Hotel on Dublin's Stephen's Green.

The Shelbourne Hotel in Dublin is one of the cities more elegant hotels. Founded by Martin Burke, a native of County Tipperary whose dream it was to open a hotel to woo the more "genteel" members of the public, who wanted a level of service fitting their needs and wanted it at a more fashionable address. Opened in 1824 and named after William Petty, 2nd Earl of Shelbourne, the hotel has played a huge part in the history of the country including during the First World War when all of its German staff were arrested. During the 1916 Rising, the British army occupied the hotel with forty troops under the command of Captain Andrews.

In 1922 the Irish constitution was drafted in one of the hotel rooms, under the leadership of Michael Collins. That room is now known as The Constitution Room.

During the 1950s the hotel saw an influx of Hollywood stars including John Wayne, James Cagney, Rock Hudson, Orson Welles, Elizabeth Taylor and Richard Burton. Maureen O'Hara became has the accolade for being the first person at the hotel to request a doggy bag from the restaurant! Grace Kelly visited and had a suite named after her whilst Peter O'Toole supposedly bathed in champagne during one memorable visit.

Outside the hotel the four lamp bearers are a constant topic of conversation. They are Egyptian Princesses and Nubian Slave girls but Dublin people have a history of renaming statues. The statue of Molly Malone is known as "The Tart with the Cart". The Anna Livis Statue and fountain that once held a prominent position on O'Connell Street was known as "The Floozy in the Jacuzzi". In keeping with this most Dublin of traditions, Dubliners have renamed these "The Last Four Virgins in Dublin".

Above, the entrance to the hotel with one of the Four Dublin Virgins holding her lamp. Photo courtesy of Stephen O'Crowley.

Oliver was spotted many times at the Shelbourne sitting in the lobby, just watching. He was happy to sign autographs and talk to anyone who approached him. One morning he sat in a chair that was probably too small for him and as he tried to get out, he needed the help of some of the hotel staff. Unfortunately as they extracted him from the chair his trousers ripped slightly. The horrified staff were very apologetic and had the trousers repaired.

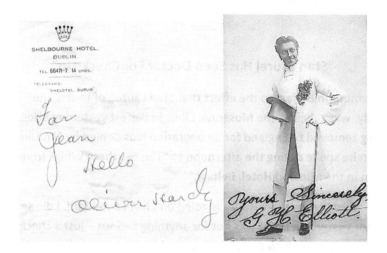

Oliver discovered that an old friend of his, G. H. Elliott was appearing onstage at the Olympia Theatre where he himself had performed a couple of weeks previously. Elliot was known as the "Chocolate Coloured Coon" and came onstage dressed totally in white and covered in black face make up. His act consisted of singing and dancing. One night Oliver and Lucille took their seats for the performance and Mr. Elliott was flabbergasted when the curtains opened and Oliver Hardy was sitting in the audience. There was a reunion after the show and all three had drinks in one of the theatre's bars.

While Oliver and Lucille were enjoying their break in Dublin, Stan was busy recuperating and catching up on his correspondence in Belfast. On June 19th, just days before he entered the clinic, he had given an interview from his suite at the Midland Hotel. The Northern Whig newspaper ran the story the next day.

"Stan Laurel Has Seen Doctor For Check-Up"

"A rumour in Belfast to the effect that Stan Laurel, of Laurel and Hardy, was taken to the Musgrave Clinic in Belfast yesterday prior to being removed to England for an operation was denied by Mr. Laurel when he spoke during the afternoon to "The Northern Whig" from his room in the Midland Hotel, Belfast."

'The show in the Opera House is going on', Mr. Laurel said. I did see a doctor yesterday, but it was not for anything serious – just a check-up. After Saturday's show I shall go into the Musgrave Clinic for another check-up, and I will probably stay there for a further week. Then I shall go to Sheffield with Mr. Hardy for the start of another show.'

"Stan Laurel had an operation in Paris some weeks ago and since then he has been on a diet."

Louis and Marie Rea were married in 1951 in Belfast. Louis was a huge fan of the Boys and his wife knew this. Thinking that a nice first anniversary present to him would be a letter from Stan and Ollie, she took it upon herself to get just that. She wrote to them at the Midland Hotel requesting an autograph but what she received back was more than she could hope for, a personal letter from Stan.

Courtesy of Louis Jnr. and Tommy Rea. With thanks to Gerry Dunne and Keith Davidson.

The letter was accompanied by one of the pre-signed cards that the Boys sometimes handed out. Closer inspection by Gerry Dunne and some sleuthing on his part, posed a question. The boys finished their Belfast shows on Saturday 21st June. Lucille and Babe probably took the

Enterprise train back down to Dublin the next day, and Stan was probably admitted to hospital on Monday 24th June. It is interesting that the letter bears the date of 24th June.

We know that during his sojourn in the Musgrave and Clarke clinic, Stan kept himself busy as usual by catching up with his correspondence. Therefore it is possible that he wrote the letter to Louis and Marie while he was in hospital. We know he made use of hotel stationary for his letters, and there are many examples of him doing just that. So, it is possible to assume that he slipped a few sheets of Midland Hotel stationery into his bag to take with him. Also, as there is no signature from Babe on the letter, it is also safe to assume that Stan wrote it after Oliver and Lucille had left for Dublin, which explains why he signed it "Laurel and Hardy". Sadly Louis passed away in 1997 but Marie and the family still treasure the little photo and the letter they received from Stan all those years ago.

"My Dear Booth [Colman] -

Sorry so long in answer yours of the 9th. inst. Haven't had much chance to get down to personal correspondence due to the exciting visit to Ireland. Being our first time here, they went ALL OUT to give us a true Irish Welcome & didn't miss a thing. Bus. as you can imagine was enormous - broke house record here (57 years) We are laying off this week so decided to go into Hospital here for rest & check up, so am able to get a chance to clean up my desk with the mail dept. away from the **maddening crowd.**"

Thankfully Stan recovered sufficiently and the Boys were reunited in time to continue their tour which took them away from Ireland and on to Sheffield.

The tour ended in October with an appearance at the New Theatre in Cardiff. Before leaving the U.K. they made a trip to London and to the Prince of Wales Theatre. Their reason, to see a rising British comedian on his eighteen month tour in "Paris to Picadilly". They had been aware of his up and coming status on their 1947 tour and here, a few years later, he had reached the heights of star status. The Boys must have held him in high regard to make the effort to see his show and it is testament to his comedy genius that they did. The comedian in question was Norman Wisdom. Behind the curtain a stagehand found Norman and told him who was out front.

Backstage at the Prince of Wales Theatre.

Norman peeked through the curtain and saw the Boys sitting four rows back in the stalls. During the interval Norman did something very rare and asked permission to go out and talk to them. When the audience saw what was happening the entire theatre erupted in cheering and applause as the three comedians clowned around.

Clowning with Norman Wisdom (Rex Features)

On October 9th, the Boys and their wives sailed away from the U.K. on board the Queen Elizabeth and back to American soil having completed a hugely successful tour.

1953 "Here We Go Again"

Life moved on for the Laurels and the Hardys. The growing popularity of television and the fact that their old short films were being shown regularly resulted in a tide of offers from all corners. There were promises of films in Japan and Australia amongst others but sadly nothing came of these offers and each promise fell through.

Stan's health was very good and he looked considerably better than he had done for many years. Oliver Hardy however had slowed down and now weighed over 300 pounds.

Writing to his friend Cingalee from his home on April 25th 1953 Stan wrote,

"Funny you should happen to mention Belfast, remember Geo. Lodge the managing director? well, he has been visiting here for a couple of weeks & is leaving for home on Monday next. We have been with him several times - lunches etc. He wanted us to play Panto this Xmas in Belfast, but Babe is not too hot about it - too much work, so that's out. However we have promised to play Variety for him when we come over again. Delfont wants us to do Panto at the London Casino this year, but am afraid that's out & if we come over in Oct. I don't know where the hell we cruld play during the Panto Season as all the variety change policy for that."

Writing to Betty Healy on June 4th, Stan wrote,

"The Australian trip has been postponed, we will have to wait till the Tax situation is cleared up or no use of us going. So now its back to England for a year & maybe by that time things will get straightened out for Australia. We open in London for eight weeks in Oct. then tour the provinces again."

In a letter to Lawrie and Jeanette Lorraine (The Singing Cartoonist) August 10th 1953 from his home in Franklin Ave. Santa Monica, Stan wrote,

"As far as the supporting Bill is concerned, that matter is entirely out of our hands, we are merely engaged for a certain period & have to play on any bill he chooses. We have nothing to say as to who we would like or dislike, we have no choice whatsoever. I can only suggest that you contact the Delfont Office & see what happens & I will personally hold good thoughts for you."

Obviously the Lorraines were hoping to tour with the Boys once more and hoped he might be able to sway some work their way. Stan continued,

"Our reason for going direct to Dublin is, we are not allowed to enter Eng. until Oct.5th. & as we

a pen the 19th. we have'nt time to get ready,
being a new act, scenery to make, rehearsals
etc. Its a nuisance, but the only way we can
manage it. We leave here this Aug.30th. sail
from New York Sept.3rd. SS "America", due in
Cobh, Eire. the 9th. then train to Dublin."

And as Stan said, they had agreed to undertake another tour of the British Isles. The reason they were not allowed enter the England was due to Oliver's working visa. He had to wait a full year to enter the country for working purposes and this would not happen until October. They decided to come to Dublin to rehearse their sketch that Stan was going to write there. It would also give them some time to relax and acclimatise due to the fact that they had struggled with this on the last trip. What they did not realise is that something was going to completely take their breath away as soon as they spied Irish soil.

"Saps (and Colleens) at Sea"

The Boys, accompanied once more by their wives Ida and Lucille, left New York on 3rd September 1953 on board the SS America for the 2960 mile trip to Cobh Harbour, County Cork, Ireland. The SS America had been launched in 1939 by Eleanor Roosevelt and had spent time as a liner before being taken over and used as a Navy Transporter during the Second World War.

After entry in World War II, the United States military was desperate for transport. Non-essential civilian ships were often temporarily employed for use by the armed services. For the *S. S. America*, the call would come whilst on cruise to Saint Thomas in the Virgin Islands. In late May of 1941 she was ordered to return to Newport News to be handed over to the Navy. The *America* was moored at Norfolk and acquired by the Navy on June 1, 1941, to be used as a troop transport. The ship was renamed the *USS West Point.*

In 1945 the *U.S.S. West Point* travelled to Italian and French ports. Its mission was to take part in the "Magic Carpet" voyages, bringing home American troops from the European battlefronts. During her naval service she would carry over 350,000 troops, the most of any Navy troopship in service during World War II.

After taking the Boys to Cobh it was sold many times and had numerous uses. It sailed between Australia, New Zealand and Southampton for a time. There were plans to convert it into a prison ship during the early 1980s but this never happened. It cruised the Mediterranean for a short time. Having experienced engine flooding it was sold for scrap although this process was halted and it was sold, with plans to convert it into a hotel ship in Thailand. In 1994 during her 100 day towing to Thailand she hit a thunderstorm and her tow crew were rescued by helicopter. On the 18th January that year she ran aground off the coast of Fuerteventura in the Canary Islands and within two days the sea had broken her. Over the next decade or so she sunk piece by piece and the wreck is now only visible at low tide.

The following newspaper article appeared in the New York Mirror on December 3rd 1951,

"STORK ADDS COLLEEN TO LINER LIST"

"The U.S. Liner America, Which left Cobh, Ireland for these shores Monday with 960 Mrs. Martin F Lacey holds her 41/2-pound daughter, Marie, born prematurely at sea aboard liner SS America. Mrs. Martin F Lacey holds her 41/2-pound daughter, Marie, born prematurely at sea aboard liner SS America. Passengers on her manifest arrived yesterday with 961–the 961st being petite winsome Marie Teresa Lacey, a 4-day-old colleen born prematurely Wednesday on the high seas.

It was the stork's first visit to the America, and Marie got a lot more attention than the VIP's aboard when the ship docked at 9am at pier 61, North River and 21st Street. Even the Immigration and Naturalization Service, which can be pretty sticky sometimes, smiled indulgently and let her come in under the visa of her mother, Mrs. Anne Lacey, a 25-year-old Irish immigrant, and with the same alien status. The moment the gangplank was lowered, the excited father, Martin F. Lacey, 32, a rigger who came to the U.S. several months ago and has been living at 436 Front Street, Dunellen, N.J., was hustled aboard by the line officials to greet his wife and take a first look at his baby.

From the standpoint of elegance, Marie's shipboard incubator wasn't up to luxury-liner standards, having been hastily improvised from a cardboard carton, previously filled with cabbages and potatoes, with a lining of menus from the dinning saloon for insulation, towels and cotton for padding, and a frame over the top through which oxygen could be fed. But it did the job, and the head waiter and three engineers who made it, under the direction of the ship's surgeon, Dr Roderick MacPherson, were proud of their handiwork. Dr MacPherson, who officiated at the delivery, was equally pleased.

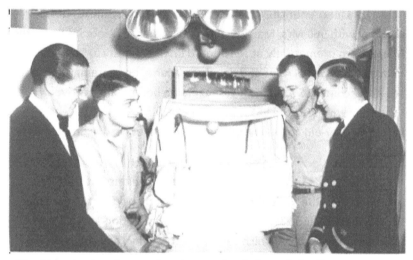

Flanking the incubator they improvised aboard the liner America for baby Marie Teresa Lacey are (left to right): Head Waiter Archie Mundy, James Francesconi, 2nd engineer; Harvey Milnar, 3rd engineer, and Joseph Belanger, 3rd assistant engineer, New York Daily Mirror December 3, 1951"

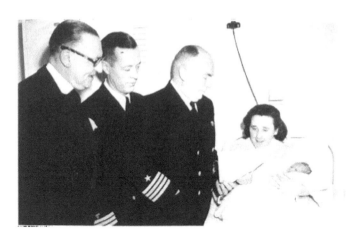

Mrs. Anne Lacey and baby Marie on board the America

©united-states-lines.org

A united-states-lines.org blog post from Larry Driscoll shows that it might have cost the Boys $350 if they took a first class passage. **"As close as I can get is 1953 Offseason/summer Southampton First $350 Cabin $220 Tourist $175"**

S.S. America in its heyday.

The SS America now sadly wrecked.

One of the many lounges on board the America.

Cobh

Cobh (pronounced "cove") is situated on the southern shore of Great Island in one of the world's finest natural harbours. Some of its early place names are believed to come from battles with Phoenician Invaders. In the 7th century it was visited by religious monks who settled there and began their secluded life of prayer. By 1176 the invasion of Henry the 2nd of England reached the port and altered the ownership and perspectives of local landowners. When Queen Victoria visited Ireland for the first time in 1849 it was here that she first set foot on Irish soil and the town was renamed Queenstown in honour of her visit. However following Irish Independence from Britain in 1920, it was renamed Cobh which is an Irish language word for Cove and is pronounced the same.

Its history is filled with great ships, majestic liners and adventurous tales of the sea. As Ireland's most strategic port of call for transatlantic liners, it became the primary port of emigration witnessing Ireland's sad emigration of its treasured sons and daughters to brighter and better things in the New World.

Many famous ships graced its shores, from the age of Sail through to the great age of Steam and into the present age of Diesel. These included the paddle steamer 'Sirius', which in 1838 became first ever ship to cross the Atlantic from the Harbour to New York without the aid of sail. The Lusitania which was torpedoed in May 1915 with the loss of 1198 lives. The troop ships that sent young men and women to conflicts such as the American War of Independence, the Boer War the Crimea War and the First World War.

Cobh, Cork was the last port of call of RMS Titanic which anchored at the mouth of the harbour on April 11th 1912. It was from here that the ship weighed anchor for the last time and sailed west towards her tragic fate in the icy waters of the North Atlantic. One hundred and twenty three passengers left form Cobh. The town has always maintained a strong maritime tradition. Today while respecting the various tragedies of the past, it shines with a vibrancy that lifts the spirit and embraces Ireland's new confidence and vision.

The statue of Annie Moore and her brothers at Cobh.

Annie Moore left Cobh on the Steamship Nevada in 1892 with her two brothers, Anthony (15) and Philip (12). Their parents had already taken the journey in order to set up home in New York. She was the first immigrant to be processed at the new Ellis Island facility and received a $10 gold piece to mark the fact. She married the son of German catholic immigrants Joseph Schayer and had at least 11 children. She died in December 1924 and in 2008 her unmarked grave in Calvary Cemetery in Queens NY, finally received a marker of Blue Irish Limestone in the shape of a Celtic Cross.

After six days at sea, the liner with Laurel and Hardy on board approached Cobh harbour off the southern coast of Ireland. As the Liner was too large to enter the harbour, it moored just off Roche's Point and the disembarking passengers were ferried to land via tenders.

As Stan and Oliver along with their wives prepared to come across, they witnessed a lot of activity on the quay. Hundreds and hundreds of people, possibly in the thousands, we really have no way of knowing, waving and shouting. Smiling at all this commotion, they had absolutely no idea it was all for them. The shock was yet to come, for it was moments later as they neared dry land and disembarked the tender that something amazing came to their ears. The great carillon bells of St. Colman's Cathedral were playing "The Cuckoo Song".

As realisation began to set in, they recognised that the shouts and cheers from the crowd were actually people shouting, "Laurel and Hardyyyyyy" over and over. This unprecedented turn out and show of affection was a welcome to Ireland that surpassed any welcome they had ever had or would experience ever again. Stan told the story afterwards that he looked at Oliver and they both simply cried.

Coming ashore was going to be difficult in the small area that was Cobh's passenger arrival area. On this day it was made all the more challenging by the throngs of well-wishers and children who just wanted to say "welcome" and "hello" to their famous visitors. They were presented with pieces of paper from people. Pieces of paper with phone numbers and addresses scribbled onto them. All with invitations to come to people's homes for dinners and drinks. A local bakery had baked a special cake in their likeness and this was somehow presented to them.

To say they were shocked is an understatement. Shocked and completely unprepared for the scene in front of them. And with scenes like that come additional problems. Eye witnesses recall Oliver Hardy being visibly shaken and frightened and who can blame him. There must have been a crowd rush of sorts and in any scenario this can be a shock. Add to the fact that a six day sea voyage was obviously tiring and could leave a person unstable and nauseous. As a result several children did not get the reaction they had hoped for from this usually courteous and funny man. One person described him as "unsmiling and discourteous towards us." The photos recorded as they came ashore that day do not show Stan Laurel. Could it be that he too was so shocked and scared at the crowd scene that he waited to come ashore?

Jasper Wilson was a local businessman and a keen photographer. He took some photographs of the pair arriving and I am indebted to his relative Stephen Wilson for the permission to reproduce them here.

The Boys on board the tender waiting to disembark. Photo with thanks from The Wilson Collection and Stephen Wilson.

Oliver Hardy looking a little worried as he makes his way through the crowd. With thanks to The Wilson Collection and Stephen Wilson.

Local man Harry Deane approached and squared up to Oliver Hardy in a fun contest to see who was the heaviest. Harry was a well-known local character and a little on the large side. Oliver Hardy, always one to take a wager, took the bet. The weighing scales at the postal depot at the port was used and Harry was declared the winner but only by a couple of pounds.

Two photos of Oliver Hardy. He seems to be happier in the second shot.
With thanks to The Wilson Collection and Stephen Wilson.

As you can see from the photographs, crowds of people are simply trying to get their moment with Laurel and Hardy. As Stan does not feature in the shots, one must assume one of two things. The Boys became separated in the confusion and the photographer Jasper Wilson was closer to Oliver. Or Stan did not disembark for one reason or another. Perhaps Lucille and Ida were frightened and he stayed with them. One thing is certain. He did eventually make it onto Irish soil.

A point to note is the fact that with thousands of people wanting to get their moment with their heroes, the small harbour town of Cobh only had a small police team and as the situation unfolding was totally spontaneous, the police were well outnumbered and not in a position to offer too much assistance. Stan said as much in a letter to his old friend Booth Coleman not long afterwards.

EIRE
Oct.5th.'53.

My Dear Booth [Colman]-

Thanks for your letter (Sept. 26.) always enjoy hearing from you. First, congratulations re the Warner Picture, am sincerely happy to hear about it & my full wishes for success in which Eda joins. Lots of good luck Booth. Yes, it is too bad. Pictures were made of our arrival in Cobh, but, as I told you it was an impromptu affair & a complete surprise to us all - as we first saw the crowds all yelling etc. - we hadn't the slightest idea what it was all about till someone on board of the Tender told us to listen to the Cathedral Bells - Then came dawn! There may have been pictures taken by individuals - There was a news photographer on the Dock when we got off - but of course all he did was in the close ups - half of them never think to photograph the crowd - only the attraction. Had we known, we could have arranged to have it properly covered - it's a shame - but just one of those things. We had dozens of letters & notes handed to us - invitations to homes etc. One pastry shop made a Big cake for us with our faces designed on it & welcome etc. but of course didn't go anywhere - Just impossible to move - was glad to get into the car & away - reminded us of our Glasgow reception in 32! & Rome in '50. at times. It's terrifying - just a mass of humanity. It's wonderful, but a terrible ordeal.

As ever-

Stan.

When the shock and commotion calmed down a little, the two comedians had one thing on their minds. The fact that the great cathedral bells had played their theme tune. How could this happen? It must have taken a lot of practice to get that rope pulling to such perfection. They insisted on thanking the bell ringers in person. With the help of Sean O'Brien, Manager of the U.S. Lines, it was explained to them that the carillon bells were not the usual type of church bell but were in fact played via a key console and not by ropes. Even more intrigued, they were guided to the safety of Mr. O'Brien's car and then taken around the small streets of Cobh and on up to the cathedral doors where Mr. Staf Gebruers, the head Carillonneur was standing.

Mr. Adrian Gebruers, Staf's son and current head Carillonneur takes up the story and my thanks to him for his input and interest in this publication.

By Adrian Patrick Gebruers KSG. Reproduced from visitcobh.com with thanks.

"It must be recorded that the Laurel and Hardy visit to Cobh in 1953 has become the most high-profile episode involving the Cobh Carillon and has spread the fame of the instrument far and wide. Almost every book about the comedians mentions it, the event was warmly recalled in the "This Is Your Life" show the following year (1954), it has been the subject of countless radio and television features and is frequently quoted in newspaper and magazine articles.

The story begins in the picture palaces of Antwerp back in the early 1920's, when my father (Staf Gebruers, 1902-1970), then a impecunious young music student, earned much needed pocket money as a temporary cinema pianist and thus was planted the seed for a life-long passion for stars of the silent screen. Fast forward to Cobh some thirty years later, where news was trickling through that Laurel and Hardy had boarded the U.S. Lines liner SS "America" in New York bound for the Emerald Isle. Whereas the duo's departure from the Big Apple had not attracted much attention, the people of Cobh were veritably tingling with excitement at the prospect of seeing them in the flesh, particularly on the part of the younger members of the population.

If the truth were to be told, the comedians were no longer that popular in the land that made them and this European campaign was an attempt to revive their waning fortunes, with Ireland being selected as a starting point.

On the morning in question, a little drama was unfolding at St Joseph's Boy's Primary School. As a ten year old pupil, I was not only a first-hand observer but very much a participant in these events. The thought that our favourite film comedians might be a stone's throw away down town while we scholars sat in our classrooms was more than any human beings could be asked to endure. We therefore took advantage of the morning yard break to petition the school principal to allow us out to see the film stars. As at that stage the ageing Br. Eugenius was probably not in the best of health, the collective pressing of hundreds of over-excited boys was probably more than he could take. Moreover, as he instinctively backed away from the onslaught we inadvertently were responsible for pressing him up against the school building, just alongside the white statue of our holy patron as it happened. In what the poor brother might well have considered to be one of his last breaths, he just about managed to gasp out the words we longed to hear: "Alright, you can go down to see them."

Housewives going about their daily shopping on The Beach, Cobh's main thoroughfare, first thought they were detecting the sound of distant thunder, but with the addition of youngster's exuberant voices it soon became obvious that the town's schoolchildren were rushing down West View hill en route to the railway station where passengers from the liners disembarked. As my best friend was Seán O'Mahony and his parents managed the Royal Cork Yacht Club, I was able to get on to the balcony of the building, which commands a fine close-up view of the harbour. When the tender taking the passengers ashore from the liner passed we waved and shouted and repeatedly rang a ship's bell in welcome, just as everyone else of the thousands lining the waterfront were similarly engaged. The two film stars were completely taken aback by the sheer ecstasy of their reception and in the years left to them never tired of reminiscing about that Wednesday, September 9 1953:

"The docks were swarming with many hundreds of people. 'It's strange, a strange thing,' Stan says in recalling that day, 'our popularity has lasted so long. Our last good pictures were made in the thirties, and you'd think people would forget, but they don't. The love and affection we found that day at Cobh was simply unbelievable. There were hundreds of boats blowing whistles and mobs and mobs of people screaming on the docks. We just couldn't understand what it was all about. And then something happened that I can never forget. All the church bells in Cobh started to ring out our theme song, and Babe looked at me, and we cried. Maybe people loved us and our pictures because we put so much love in them. I don't know. I'll never forget that day. Never".

When the two celebrities stepped ashore in Cobh they were immediately surrounded by good humoured milling crowds, all wishing to catch a glimpse of them or even shake their hands or get an autograph. The few local Gardaí fought a losing battle to speed them through immigration and customs formalities and out to a waiting car, and there was some considerable delay before they eventually emerged from the railway station to more cheering masses of fans. Ollie did not look a well man that morning, but in spite of how he might have been feeling he and Stan were insisting on personally thanking "the bell-ringers". Like most people, they knew next to nothing about carillons and even less of how they're played. When Seán O'Brien, manager of the U. S. Lines and a personal friend of my father's, explained that this was an instrument played from a keyboard by one man they were even more anxious to make his acquaintance. A few minutes later, Seán's car sped around Cathedral Corner followed Pied-Piper like by hundreds of screaming children.

My father was at the main entrance, where I had joined him standing shyly a few steps behind. My first reaction was one of disappointment as these two elderly gentlemen dressed in modern lounge suits alighted, only vaguely resembling their far more familiar screen personae. But even worse confusion was to follow. When Ollie went to take my father's hand to thank him the accumulated emotion of that whole morning seemed to suddenly spill over the poor man and words failed him. Tears began to roll down his cheeks as he engulfed Dad in his not inconsiderable embrace. Alarmed that my father, who in these politically-correct days would be termed vertically-challenged, might not come out intact from that massive bear hug, I was even more unnerved by Stan's contrasting total composure as, dry eyed, he repeated polite words of appreciation. Shouldn't he be the distraught one, wringing his hands and bawling crying as Ollie yet again admonishes: "That's another fine mess you've gotten us into.", when in fact the reverse seemed to be the case! But there was no denying the sincerity of the film stars' gratitude.

Having their theme played on the Carillon and the great warmth of the welcome they'd witnessed in Cobh was a genuine public acknowledgment of the innocent fun they had given to millions which seemed to deeply touch them and was to become a landmark experience in their twilight years."

Above, a young Adrian turns the sheet music for his father at the organ. Courtesy of Adrian Gebruers. Photographer Liam Kennedy

Liam Muldowney and Adrian Gebruers in 2019 just before our appearance on Irish daytime television. From the author's collection

Work began on the fabulous building that would become St. Colman's in 1868 but it was not completed until almost fifty years later due to increasing building costs and revised architectural plans. It was finally consecrated on August 24th 1919 by Robert Browne, Archbishop of Cloyne.

Above, St. Colmans Cathedral, Cobh standing majestically over the port of Cobh. Photo by Jaqueline Banerjee, http://www.victorianweb.org/art/architecture/puginew/1.html

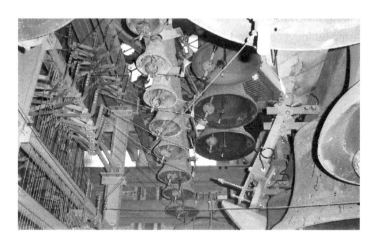

The inner workings of the Carillon Bells

An Echo Newspaper reporter commented thus, **"The entire children's population of Cobh must have played truant from school for they blocked all traffic and despite the presence of several vastly amused policemen, they clung to Laurel and Hardy. They begged for autographs, ruffled their ties and generally gave them a wholehearted reception. Nonplussed but only for a moment, the comedians entered into the fun of the affair and no one could accuse them of being stinted in giving autographs. Twenty three stone Hardy, 22st 12lb to be exact, commented, *'we were absolutely overwhelmed. There scarcely ever was a film scene like it. They are grand children and Stan and I are grateful to them.'***

From Cobh the Boys and their wives were driven to Cork City Hall where they were met by the Lord Mayor, Alderman Patrick McGrath. He welcomed them handsomely to the city and invited them inside for a civic reception.

The photographs that exist from the day show the utter happiness in the mayor's face. Meeting the two men meant so much to him as it turned out that he was a huge fan of their films.

Alderman P. McGrath with the Boys at Cork City Hall. Echo Newspapers and www.irishnewspaperarchives.com

Above, The Visitor's Book from Cork City Hall

The photo includes Sean O'Brien and A.A. Healy, a local politician. At the back Lucille Hardy is second from left and Ida Laurel is far right.
www.irishnewspaperarchives.com

The party were taken to see one of Ireland's greatest attractions, The Blarney Stone. The Blarney Stone is a block of Carboniferous limestone built into the battlements of Blarney Castle, Blarney, about 8 kilometres (5 miles) from Cork. According to legend, kissing the stone endows the kisser with *the gift of the gab* (great eloquence or skill at flattery). The stone was set into a tower of the castle in 1446. The castle is a popular tourist site in Ireland, attracting visitors from all over the world to kiss the stone and tour the castle and its gardens. Kissing the stone involves lying on your back and bending backwards over an open space, then pressing your lips against a piece of rock that has been kissed by thousands of lips over the years!

Courtesy of Blarney Castle Visitor's Attraction

In order to kiss the stone one must first ascend to the top of the tower via a set of steps and a narrow stairway. Oliver Hardy made the decision not to climb the steps, more than likely due to his size and because of the amount of energy required to do so. Today the attraction makes a point of telling visitors that he did actually ascend the steps and negotiate the small stairway as a way of alleviating any apprehension one might have about the task.

Many of you may be here to kiss the Blarney Stone and to gain the gift of eloquence. You will be following in historic footsteps. As long ago as 1789, the French Consul to Dublin wrote of 'Blarney Castle on the top of which is a large stone that visitors who climb up are made to kiss..."

You will learn more of the story of the Stone as you pass through the Castle chambers. Take care as you mount the winding stairs and, if you think that the way is narrow, consider that two who went before you were Oliver Hardy and Winston Churchill. Eloquence is not just a gift for the sylph-like.

Courtesy of Blarney Castle Visitor's Attraction

Stan, Ida and Lucille climbed the steps to the kiss the stone with Oliver staying below and giving the reason that "no one would hold me, I'm too big."

**Stan (in light coloured suit), readies himself to kiss the stone.
Courtesy Evening Echo Newspapers.**

From Blarney the Boys were taken to the train station to say their goodbyes to the Cork people and their hosts for the day including Mr. Sean O'Brien. Truth told they were probably happy to board the train to Dublin and the chance to have a few hours to themselves.

The Irish Examiner of September 10th reported the Cobh docking as follows,

"The famous comedy team of Stan Laurel and Oliver Hardy were scheduled to disembark from the liner America which called at Cobh yesterday from New York. No elaborate reception was planned and the shipping officials carried out the usual arrangements for the arrival of important passengers. The famous pair wanted no fuss and of course the liner company officials were anxious to carry out to the letter the wishes of their first class passengers."

This has been the story told of the arrival of Laurel and Hardy into Cobh. They wanted no fuss, no advance warning of their arrival. However, this was not the case. No matter how the newspapers reported it.

How did the children know they were on board the America? Did the cake shop just happen to have a cake made in their image? If nothing had been arranged, why did they go willingly to Blarney and Cork City Hall to a reception?

The people of Cork did know they were coming. The trip to kiss the Blarney Stone was pre-arranged. As was the reception with the Lord Mayor at City Hall.

The Examiner Newspaper of September 5th (four days before they docked) reported,

"The United States Lines vessel America with nine hundred passengers from New York is due on Wednesday to land 110 passengers and 1523 sacks of mail and embark 100 cross-channel passengers, the latter including a part of forty on pilgrimage to Lourdes and Lisieux.

Passengers to land will include Mr. and Mrs. Oliver M. (sic) Hardy and Mr. and Mrs. Stan Laurel. Messers Laurel and Hardy, the famous comedians together with their wives will make a brief tour of Cobh, Cork and Blarney before proceeding to Dublin."

Dun Laoghaire

Stan and Oliver's arrival in Dublin could not have been more modest following their rapturous welcome in Cobh and the civic reception at Cork City Hall. The train from Kent Station in Cork would have taken approx. three and a half hours, ensuring them a little time to catch their breath. With memories of the previous year's tour still fresh in their minds, they must have felt some trepidation about arriving in Ireland's capital city where they been so warmly welcomed fifteen months before. Add to that their almost prisoner like existence in Belfast and the now unbelievable experiences at Cobh, what on Earth was Dublin going to be like.

They need not have worried. They caught the 3.15pm express train service to Dun Laoghaire with a ten minute stop at Dublin's Heuston Station. When the train pulled into Dun Laoghaire Pier Station at 8.15pm it was late evening and well past tea time in the city. As they were not scheduled to play any dates in the capital and so their arrival was unannounced and very low key due to the fact that the public weren't aware they were coming in the first place. They were spotted by a disbelieving passenger who thought he was seeing things as he looked down the platform to see Laurel and Hardy struggling with an enormous trunk. Firstly that it could actually be them and secondly that they were having to look after their own luggage without a single piece of help.

The Boys and their wives were booked into The Royal Marine Hotel, a charming Victorian hotel situated in Dun Laoghaire, a harbour port which was a ten mile car journey from the city centre. Their arrival at the hotel was quiet and without fanfare. The Irish Times newspaper happened to know they were in town and a reporter was dispatched to the hotel. It was quite late in the day and when he arrived he spotted Stan and Ida Laurel having dinner.

Ever the gentleman, Stan was happy to talk to him and the next day's edition reported as follows.

"The two couples arrived in Dublin virtually unnoticed. Last night when an Irish Times reporter visited the Royal Marine Hotel, Dun Laoghaire, where they are staying, he found Stan Laurel and his wife at dinner. "Olly is resting", said Stan. "We had a terrific heat wave in New York before we left, and well, it was just too much for him. He did not quite get over it until a few days out on the boat, and then the journey…." Stan and Oliver will rest until Monday morning when they will be joined by a scriptwriter from London. For the following fortnight they will think up scripts for their show. "We are thinking of calling it Birds of a Feather but we may change that title", Laurel said. Their show will go on a 12 months tour of British theatres. "We will be appearing in Belfast but I do not know about Dublin yet."

The cast which will take part in the show will arrive in Dublin in a fortnight's time and will rehearse in the Olympia Theatre, Dublin where the two comedians appeared last year during their first visit to Ireland. The scenery for the show is being made in Belfast and will be brought to Dublin for the rehearsals. Laurel and Hardy would have rehearsed in England but for some labour restrictions which prevent them from going there until October.

"But we are very pleased to be in Ireland", Stan Laurel said. "Cobh was a lovely place and from what I have seen of Dun Laoghaire (he had some trouble with the pronunciation of both names) it seems to be a beautiful spot."

The visa restrictions were down to Oliver Hardy having left Britain at the end of September the previous year. As mentioned, he had to wait a full twelve months to return. The Boys were never scheduled to appear in Belfast despite Stan's newspaper interview. It is highly probable that transport was booked with the plan to include Dublin and Belfast. With several theatres in both cities, it is also probable that these were already booked with other acts and not available, as a letter from Stan, written in Dun Laoghaire shows.

> *Sept.12.'53.*
> *Dear Dorothi & Jac [Bock Pierre]-*
> *Just recd. your kind "Bye Card" - evidently missed the boat & was forwarded on. Thanks for the sweet thought.*
> *Had a nice crossing - calm sea all the way. Eda caught a cold so is now in the Pill & nose drops dept. Lovely Hotel here - nice large room & Bath facing the harbour & food good. Had quite a reception in Cork - looked like the whole Town turned out to greet us & the Cathedral Bells played our Cuckoo Song. It was really a sight. Drove to Cork - received by the Lord Mayor at the City Hall & then taken to see Blarney Castle & the famous Stone. Then got on the train & autographed our way to Dublin! A sure hectic way.*
> *We were up at 5:30.am. The ship anchored at 7. & we came into Cork on a Tender to be*

pushed around all day! We start to work Monday - so glad to have a few days rest. We arrived in New York during that awful heat wave (102) that was really terrible! Mr. Murphy arrived at the Boat loaded down with Pepsicola, pens & pencils and a couple of very important Gents who can get us through the Customs when we return without inspection!!! Will let you know when we are coming back so you can bail us out! What a guy! Bob Hope is playing in Dublin for a couple of nights - too tired to go & see the show. All for now.

Eda joins in love & bestest - will write you again when the show opens.

Bye & God Bless.

As ever-

The Boys were spotted several times sitting on a bench at the entrance to the pier simply enjoying the sea air and watching the day go by. The Dun Laoghaire residents were often amazed as they went about their business and walked past these two giants of the screen. Disbelief lead to some members of the public approaching them and actually asking the question, "is it really you?"

Famous Irish Playwright Brendan Farrell recalled the time his father came home from work one day, gathered the children around and told them he had just met Laurel and Hardy sitting on a bench at Dun Laoghaire Pier and had a short conversation with them. He had been amazed that Stan's hair was in fact auburn in colour and not black as they had assumed due to only ever seeing him in black and white films. Bernard Farrell worked in Dun Laoghaire at the Mail Boat Pier and had seen many famous people over the years as they disembarked the boats from Wales. Jimmy Cagney, James Mason, world boxing champion Gene Tunney and even the hangman Albert Pierrepoint.

But it was the meeting with Laurel and Hardy that interested the children the most. Memories of watching them in the Astoria Cinema in Glasthule had ensured that these two comedians held a special part in the hearts of the Farrell children. "What did you say to them?" they asked. Bernard Farrell said he had been cycling by and saw the two men sitting on the bench just watching the world go by. He had stopped and doubled back and approached them. Holding out his hand he simply greeted them with, "Welcome to Ireland." Oliver Hardy smiled and replied, "Why thank you."

As the years went by the story of the meeting was retold many times. Eventually Bernard told them that "Welcome to Ireland" was actually the entire conversation he had with Stan and Oliver that day as he had then mounted his bicycle and made his way home.

ROYAL MARINE HOTEL LETTERHEAD - Dublin, Ireland - HANDWRITTEN

Sept.18th.'53.

My Dear Booth [Colman]-

Thanks yours of the 14th.inst. Had nice smooth crossing, but prefer the Cunard Line to the "America" ship, altho' its very good, but there seems to be something missing somehow. A wonderful reception on our

arrival in Cobh, seemed like everybody turned out to meet us as we came in on a tender, people came out in row boats, boat whistles blowing, the Cathedral chimes playing the Cuckoo, the schools had specially closed so the kids could be there with the cheering crowds. I never saw such a sight, this was all on the level, no publicity stunt. I have since had a letter from a guy at the Bank of Ireland there, telling me that all the staff, due to the excitement, left the bank wide open to come and see us, then realising, they all rushed back! can you imagine. It was murder getting through the crowds to our cars, the police force being small & unable to handle them (5000.Population). We were driven to Cork & taken to the City hall to meet the Lord Mayor - photos etc. & to see Blarney Castle & the Blarney Stone. We then autographed our way to Dublin. Hotel very nice here & weather so far, good. Am busy getting the script in shape to start rehearsals on the 28th when the cast arrives.

Have nice large room & bath facing the harbour (used to be Kingstown).

Eda is going to add a few lines, so will close. Trust alls well & Happy & prospects look good. Bye Booth. God bless.

As ever-

Stan.

Mrs. Laurel added to Stan's letter,

"Well, I still have the cold—and little bit lonely. Stan is busy, so I left to myself and I can't do much. All the theatre in Dublin, just like in Los Angeles. I have not any friends to go with me, I wish you were here—will be very nice. Well Booth wish you the best of everything." Love—Ida.

As Stan was working hard trying to perfect a stage show worthy of their name, it appears that Ida was at somewhat of a loose end. Lucille did accompany her on several trips into the city by car to go shopping. On one occasion, they returned to the hotel with so many shopping bags that the taxi driver had to ask the porters for extra help in unloading the car.

Oliver and Lucille lost no time filling in any spare time they had by exploring the surrounding counties and the wonderful scenery that Ireland had to offer. They took a car trip one day, a few miles south to County Wicklow. There they visited the famous Mount Usher Gardens located in Ashford. Laid out in 1868 they are still believed to be the earliest and finest example of a "Robinsonian" garden in the world. The combination of fine trees and shrubs together with floral displays gathered in informal planting schemes make it one of Ireland's top hidden tourist attractions to this day. It is easy to see how the relaxed setting would appeal to the Hardy's after the heat of New York and the hectic crossing.

Having had their fill of the beauty and smells of Mount Usher, they travelled the short drive to Hunter's Hotel where they enjoyed afternoon tea. Operating as an Inn since the 1770s this beautiful building has been in the hands of the Hunter family for almost 200 years. It still operates as a hotel today and as one enters its surroundings, the experience is as if you have stepped back in time to a simpler world.

Above is the entry in the Visitor's Book at Hunter's Hotel. Reproduced with their kind permission. Looking at the entry at the top, Irish actor Barry Fitzgerald, star of The Quiet Man missed Oliver Hardy by a number of days. With thanks to Hunter's Hotel.

As the Boys were staying for quite a while in Dun Laoghaire, Stan took the opportunity to revisit Dr. Smith in Belfast, the doctor who had stabilised his diabetes a year before. Nurse Minnie Rea remembers Stan returning to the Royal Victoria Hospital and specifically asking to be seen by the same nurses and doctors. He spent at least one night back in their care having a full check-up before returning back to Dublin.

Irish tweed had been produced in the country for generations. Originally a cottage industry, it involved entire families spinning, dyeing and spinning local wool into the fine material that is still much sought after to this day. Oliver Hardy had thought of owning a genuine Irish tweed suit for some time. His trip to Dublin the previous year did not allow the time or circumstances to have achieved this but now, here we was with time on his hands and he was not going to miss his chance. When Stan heard of his plans, he decided to join his partner and together they took the trip into Dublin to see the tailor that had been recommended to them, Louis Copeland. Still one of Ireland's master tailors, the business is now operated by Louis' son, also Louis.

The Boys had their suits made to measure, Stan choosing a suit made, not from tweed but from regular wool. Oliver on the other hand was here for a reason and he got his suit. Louis was not one to miss an opportunity and asked them if they would be part of an advertising campaign for the business. They agreed but had one stipulation. Their fee had to go to a charity. A charity they had read about some days before in the Irish newspapers and had been touched by.

The Irish Times of September 23rd ran the following story.

Laurel and Hardy give 50 Guineas to hospital fund

"A recent paragraph in The Irish Times prompted Laurel and Hardy, film and stage comedians to hand over a cheque for fifty guineas yesterday to the "Little Willie" fund which supports the Auxiliary

Orthopaedic Hospital, Baldoyle. Mr. Hardy, Oliver to his fans said yesterday that when they read about the fund in The Irish Times, he and his partner decided they could not support a better cause. The cheque was handed by Mr. Hardy to "Little Willie" himself who was accompanied by "Little Margaret". These two four year olds have been patients at the hospital since infancy.

Representing the hospital were Mrs. W. J. Mulholland, a member of the building fund committee and nurse Mary Wade. The comedians have been staying at the Royal Marine Hotel, Dun Laoghaire for a fortnight. They are combining a holiday with writing a script for a sketch which they will take on tour of the English provinces soon."

And so, on a pre-arranged date, a photo opportunity was arranged at the Royal Marine Hotel and Little Willie and Little Margaret were taken along to receive the cheque. Not a lot is known about Margaret sadly, but Willie O'Reilly (aka "Little Willie") was the mascot of a massive fund-raising campaign initiated by the Sisters of Charity in Baldoyle in the early 1950s. As a photogenic symbol of all polio-damaged children, complete with callipers and crutches, Willie was brought out on big occasions like All-Ireland Football Finals and St. Patrick's Day Parades to raise money for a new hospital. Willie had been left at the door of the convent in Baldoyle by his unmarried mother. He already had polio at only a few months of age.

He lived in Baldoyle Convent and Hospital for seventeen years, and still lives in Dublin. He remembers nothing of the day with Stan and Ollie.

www.irishnewspaperarchives.com

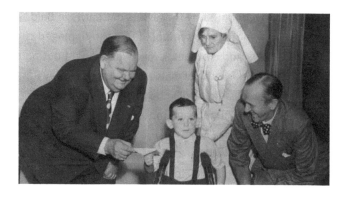

Nurse Mary Wade looks on as Oliver Hardy presents the cheque to Little Willie, above and below with the recipient.
www.irishnewspaperarchives.com

Willie O'Reilly and the Boys. www.irishnewsarchive.com

The advert in question. With thanks to Antony and Joanne Mitchell Waite

On September the 18th the Boys made a trip to the Bank of Ireland in Dun Laoghaire and took charge of £300 that was wired from the offices of Bernard Delfont in London.

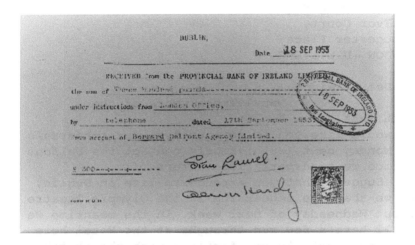

The Bank of Ireland building in George's St. Dun Laoghaire still operating as a bank today.

With the sketch progressing well, Stan wrote to Gordon Craig who was going to be assisting them in its performance.

Royal Marine Hotel
                DUN LAOGHAIRE.Co.DUBLIN.
                EIRE. SEPT. 22nd.'53.

Gordon Craig Esq.,
92,Ivor Court,
Gloucester Place,
LONDON. N.W.1.ENG.

My Dear Craig:-
                Many thanks yours of the
19th.inst.
We would like you to join us here for rehearsals
on Monday next (28th) kindly contact the Delfont
office re transportation matters.
        Suggest that you arrange to live in Dublin,
as we shall be rehearsing at the Olympia Theatre
about Wednesday of next week. In the meantime we
shall have a few run throughs at the Hotel here
with the cast, to get familiar with the sketch.
It is about six miles from here to Dublin &
there is bus or train service.
        Re the costumes & wig, we prefer to have
them purchased, regulation Nurses outfit, blue
with white collar & cuffs & white cap. The wig I
will leave up to you, whatever you are
accustomed to working in. Get two outfits & have
charged to L&H, Delfont office. Will appreciate
if you will bring them with you.
        Thank you for your kind wishes.
                Sincerely
always:-

From the letter, we can see that Stan was very much in charge of the performance. His tone regarding the costume shows just how much of a perfectionist he was. Everything that Gordon Craig needed to know was covered in that letter including his transportation, living arrangements and who to see regarding expenses. Proof that Stan really was in control.

During his days at Roach he took charge and headed the team of gagmen. When shooting started he was known to take over and the directors were quite happy to let him, knowing that Stan knew what he was doing and was not simply taking over for the sake of it. They knew that there was no big-headedness when it came to Stan. He never played the "I am the famous actor" card. Stan just would not settle for anything less than perfect or as perfect as it could be. Even Roach knew this and rarely interfered.

The Irish Times newspaper had a supplemental magazine called the Pictorial that was issued every Wednesday. Every week, the staff had an in house competition to see who could come up with the best cover photo and in mid- September 1953, they were stuck. As they sat around their desks trying to come up with ideas, one member of staff remarked that Laurel and Hardy were in town. Without hesitation, they headed for Dun Laoghaire and found Stan and Oliver only too delighted to help out.

It was decided that having the Boys do what they do best was going to be the most exciting cover photo. Ollie being Ollie and Stan at his best, being Stan. A quick trip to the local newsagents around the corner on Marine Road found that a surplus of biscuit tins were available. These were quickly wrapped in brown paper and taken to the front of the hotel where the photographs were taken. Reproduced here courtesy of The Irish Times and photographer Dermot Barry.

Above, "empty biscuit tins Stanley" Photographer Dermot Barry

Above, The cover of the magazine. Courtesy Irish Times. Photographer Dermot Barry

Above, another photograph from the shoot. Irish Times Newspapers. Photographer Dermot Barry. Thanks to Colin Howe.

Also taken at the same shoot, The Boys in front of the Royal Marine Hotel. Photographer Dermot Barry

One Laurel and Hardy fan who wasn't going to miss the chance of meeting her heroes was fifteen year old Cora Kelly. With the help of her sister she wrote to the Royal Marine and asked if it would be possible to meet Laurel and Hardy. Two days later she received a reply and was told to be at the hotel at 3pm the next day. Cora said it was like a dream come true and nervous though she was, she arrived as arranged with her baby brownie camera. When the Boys came out to her she held her nerve and they spent almost half an hour talking to her. One of the porters kindly took the photo and Cora, now Cora Walby, treasures it to this day.

Below, Cora meeting the Boys and today, still proud of her photo.

Joe, one of the porters in the hotel was a fan of the Boys and he was not going to miss his chance at meeting the Boys and asked Cora to take one of him too.

Left, Joe and the Boys outside the Royal Marine Hotel.

Stan continued to work on the sketch and made progress each day. Lucille and Ida took several more trips into Dublin to go shopping amongst the grand Georgian architecture of the city. Oliver and Lucille were often seen sitting in the large front garden of the hotel enjoying the views of the harbour and watching the boats go about their business. The Dublin Mail Boat made daily trips to the U.K. and Oliver commented that he could almost set his watch to it.

In a letter to a friend back in the U.S. Oliver wrote, **"Dun Laoghaire is such a relaxing place. I could almost live here. The only problem is that you can't get a drop of decent Bourbon in this town."**

The Boys became part of the community for a while and through their walks and bench sitting habits, Dun Laoghaire accepted them as one of their own. They happily signed autographs and spoke with anyone who approached them.

Declan Murray was nine years old at the time and a huge fan. His mother and father were at a function in the hotel when they saw Stan Laurel in the foyer. Knowing how much an autograph would mean to her son, Mrs. Murray approached him and asked for one.
Stan sent a porter to get some paper and he returned with a piece of hotel paper. Stan duly signed it to Declan. But his mother thought that he needed Ollie's as well and asked Stan if Oliver was close by. Stan replied that he was resting but when Mrs. Murray looked slightly saddened but also accepting of the fact, Stan asked her to wait just there. He got out of his chair and went upstairs, returning a little later with a new piece of paper with both signatures on it. Declan was probably the luckiest boy in town that day, receiving two autographs.

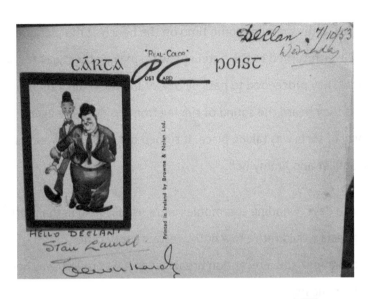

One day, after spending some time on the bench at the pier, Stan and Oliver returned to the hotel and were making their way to their rooms. They proceeded to pass by one of the hotel function rooms and as they heard the sound of singing from inside, were aware that a party of sorts was taking place. It turned out to be the wedding of Rita Sadlier and Jimmy Bell.

In those days, wedding ceremonies were usually held in the morning and guests would retire to a hotel, restaurant or other establishment and a reception breakfast as it was called, was held for their guests.

On this occasion, the guests were enjoying a sing-song around a piano which was located at the back of the room. Hearing the singing and possibly looking for a bit of diversion, the two comedians stood at the door and looked inside. It did not take too long before one of the guests spotted them and seeing that this was the case, Oliver Hardy asked would they mind if he and Stan joined them and of course they were welcomed inside.

Oliver proceeded to sit at the piano and tickle the ivories whilst entertaining the guests with his soft singing voice.

The party continued for quite some time and I'm sure that Stan didn't get to work on the sketch too much that day. I'm told they thoroughly enjoyed the wedding reception and stayed for quite a long time mingling with guests and singing and dancing.

The distraction from the pressure of work and tiring schedule ahead of them was probably something that both men badly needed.

As this was going on, the hotel enacted a special arrangement they had with the Irish Press newspaper whereby they were paid a gratuity if they tipped off the paper when something special was happening. A photographer was dispatched and when he arrived he arranged a photo opportunity with two of the bride's nieces, Noeleen Fagan and Audrey Smith. These two young ladies probably had no idea who the two men were but over time the realisation of the two very famous knees that they were sitting on has hit home and both are very proud of the photo.

Noeleen sat on Oliver's knee and enjoyed having her photograph taken with such fuss whilst her cousin Audrey was the shyer of the two and was not as interested in sitting on a strange man's knee. The deal with the hotel was, that they were not to release the photograph to the public until the Boys had left Irish soil.

It is reproduced below with thanks to Noeleen and Audrey and also Noeleen's husband Frank who contacted me and invited me to their home to meet them.

**The Boys with their special Veil Girls, Noeleen and Audrey.
Strictly copyrighted to Noeleen Reid.**

Imagine for a moment Oliver Hardy singing "You are the Ideal of my Dreams" at the piano at an Irish wedding. One can only speculate about the occasion but I would imagine that copious amounts of drinks were bought, with thanks, for the two gate crashers. One hell of a story to tell any future children and grandchildren of the happy couple.

Stan had completed the finishing touches to the sketch. A part of the act required the use of a couple of pigeons. These would form the ending of the piece where it all descends into chaos. Pigeons were possibly chosen due to their "homing" ability and the fact that they could be re-captured each evening. Performing the act every night and not being able to re-use the birds would mean an endless supply of pigeons in order to complete their engagements in Britain. Once more, Stan was in control, even sourcing birds, as his letter to old friend Claude "Cingalee" shows.

Olympia Theatre
DUBLIN. EIRE.
September 28th.'53

Dear Claude [Cingalee]:-
Many thanks yours of the 23rd.inst.
Appreciate very much, getting the pigeons for us & will let you know re the shipping of them as soon as we get to England. We expect to leave here about Oct.12th. but do'nt open until the 19th. New Theatre Northampton. On Oct.11th. we are going to break the act in at the Olympia here, a benefit matinee for the Red Cross, & we are getting a couple of pigeons here for the one show, so no use sending yours over, besides there may be difficulty bringing them in, remember you had some trouble last time you were here?.

We start rehearsals on Wednesday with the cast, so going to be plenty busy for the next two weeks.

The Boys found themselves back at the Olympia Theatre for the rehearsals. The theatre had found itself without bookings for a week and Stan was only too delighted to accept an invitation from Stanley Illsley and Leo McCabe to rehearse there. As Stan's letter to Cingalee states, it was suggested that a charity show could be organised with Laurel and Hardy as headliners to test the new sketch. Stan agreed and began the process of fine tuning the all new "Birds of a Feather" stage show. The Irish Red Cross were to be the beneficiaries of the show with monies also going to the fund to build a new catholic church in Clonskeagh, South Dublin.

The Irish Times reported on the 9th October.

"On Sunday for example – Laurel and Hardy - as a preliminary to their English tour – will stage their new playlet "Birds of a feather" at the Olympia for the Irish Red Cross and the building fund of a church at Clonskeagh. And a number of other people are going out of their way to help. Belfast born soprano Anne Jamison, now a star of American radio, is flying back from London just for the day; Billy Banks the star of the "Jolson Memories" show and Billy Rose's famous "Diamond Horse-Shoe" Club in New York has switched planes to delay his return to London in order to appear; and among the local artists there is Paddy Crosbie, who is due at a show in Graignamanagh on the same night – he'll do his part and head for his other engagement. That is the sort of thing which is at the heart of show business."

Stan Laurel and Oliver Hardy being the generous unselfish men they were did not even have to think twice about giving their time to such a charitable cause as The Red Cross. And on top of that, the Irish Catholic Church was also going to benefit.

The Clonskeagh area of Dublin was on the south of the city and in the early 1950s was experiencing something of a change. The city was spreading outwards and Clonskeagh was one of those many areas going through a building boom of new housing estates and an influx of young families moving into them. The Catholic Church held a superior position in Irish society and needed to ensure this continued through its church building programme which pin-pointed these new communities and ensured that their spiritual needs were looked after.

This building programme that Archbishop John Charles McQuaid had set up for targeted areas proved very successful. The church that Laurel and Hardy helped to fund was eventually built with Archbishop McQuaid holding a competition to design it. Specifications were that it had to accommodate seventeen hundred people and cost no more that £150,000.

The Royal Institute of Architects received a record 101 submissions. All of the shortlisted proposals were of a modernist design but very mysteriously, the building that was eventually selected was not one of them. "Irish Modernism" published in 2009, describes how McQuaid established a committee to purge designs for ultra-modern church designs. So it seems that the Archbishop vetoed the plan for a modernist church in Clonskeagh with a red bricked revivalist building being constructed instead.

The church is still in use today and lies in a more affluent area of Dublin. Its community is regarded as one of the larger church communities. I contacted them regarding their famous building fund contributors and they were quite taken aback. I was told that special prayers would be said for Stan Laurel and Oliver Hardy.

The Miraculous Medal Church in Clonskeagh.
Built with the help of Stan and Ollie.

OLYMPIA THEATRE

TO-NIGHT: 2 Shows, 6 and 8.30.
"Memories of Jolson"
NEXT WEEK (For one week)
London Star EMRYS JONES in
"DIAL 'M' FOR MURDER"
The Thriller Now Sweeping the World!
Stalls: 8 6, 6/-. Circle: 7/6, 5/-, 3/6
Now Booking 10.30 to 9 p.m.
TO-MORROW, AT 3 P.M.

LAUREL & HARDY
In Person. CHARITY SHOW
in aid of Red Cross and new Catholic
Church (Clonskeagh) Fund.
Seats available at 6/-, 7/6, 8/6 Gallery 2/-.

OCTOBER 19th (One Week)
The Season's Theatrical Highlight!
PAMELA BROWN, PAUL
SCOFIELD and GLADYS COOPER
in "A QUESTION OF FACT"
First pre-London Tennent Production to
come to Ireland!
BOOKING NOW OPEN.
Stalls: 10/-, 12 6. Circle: 5/-, 6 6, 8/6.

NEXT SUNDAY AT 3 P.M.
Two-Way Charity Show
in aid of the Irish Red Cross
and the new Catholic Church
(Clonskeagh) fund.

LAUREL
AND
HARDY
IN PERSON
in the first production of
BIRDS OF A FEATHER
and ON THE SCREEN in
WAY OUT WEST
Also first European appearance
of
ANN JAMISON
America's star radio soprano.
Now Booking at Stage Door
Office, Olympia Theatre, 10.30
to 6.
Stalls: 8/6, 6/6; Circle, 7/6,
6/-, 4/-.

LAUREL AND HARDY (in person) — Charity Show to-morrow at 3 p.m. With Anne Jamison, America's Radio Star; Billy Banks, Negro star singer; Paddy Crosbie, Freddie Doyle, Elizabeth Carroll, Nell Phelan, Eddie Lambert, Capitol Girls; Olympia Orchestra, Guest Conductor, Reg Alvis, Accompanist, Kitty O'Callaghan. In aid of Red Cross and new Catholic Church (Clonskeagh) Fund. Seats still available at 6/6, 7/6, and 8/6. Gallery, 2/-.

The Supporting Acts

N.Y.Age –7/16/32p6

Billy Banks, Jazz singer. Billy was invited by Irving Mills in 1932 to record with a group of multiracial musicians including Fats Waller and Tommy Dorsey under the name Billy Bank's Rhythmmakers. He worked as a showman and singer with Luis Russell's band and later worked with Noble Sissle. From 1938 to 1951 he appeared in cabaret shows by Billy Rose, like his Diamond Horseshoe; then he settled in England in 1952 where recordings with Freddy Randall's Orchestra were made. In the 1950s he toured Europe, Australia and East Asia. In 1954 an album was made in Denmark with Cy Laurie. In the late 1950s he moved to Japan where he died in 1967 in Tokyo.

Anne Jamison, Belfast born Soprano: Anne took over the presenting duties for The Electric Hour on CBS from Nelson Eddy. Of interest to Laurel and Hardy fans is the fact that Felix Knight appeared on the show in 1940s. Felix starred with the Boys in Babes in Toyland. Anne was known to Stan and Oliver and had been holidaying in Ireland when she heard of the show. She cut short her onward trip to England to come back to perform.

Paddy Crosbie, Irish composer, singer and comic rhyming actor. Best known for his song "School around the Corner" Paddy wrote scripts for

amateur players with such success that he was soon writing plays for Noel Purcell and the Capital Theatre. In 1951 he perfected his schoolboy act in which he would come on stage in short trousers and a school cap. This was most likely the act he performed as part of the charity show with Laurel and Hardy. Paddy went on to head his own show on Irish radio, "The School around the Corner", where he would go into Dublin's schools and chat with the children, sometimes with hilarious results.

Freddie Doyle, Comedian. Freddie was a regular on the Dublin stage for almost thirty years. He was an all-round entertainer who could incorporate comedy, impressions and hilarious routines into a very popular act. He was a regular on the Irish pantomime stage for decades.

Elizabeth Carroll, Operatic Soloist and Soprano. Elizabeth was also a well-known theatrical performer in Ireland. She appeared in a leading role in the stage production of "The Bohemian Girl" in May 1955 in Dublin. This opera by Balfe was in the Boys filmography and was released in 1936.

Neil Phelan, Magician. Known on the Dublin stage for many years, Neil was the Secretary of the Society of Irish Magicians and well respected within the society. He wore a top hat and cloak and frequently had audiences in awe as he performed a disappearing act where he vanished from the stage and reappeared in an instant at the back of the theatre (thanks to his twin brother).

The Capitol Theatre Dancers. Also known as "The Capitol Girls" under the leadership of Dolly Sparkes and Norah Flanagan, they were regulars at the nearby Capitol Theatre and gladly gave their services for the special charity show.

Eugene Lambert, Ventriloquist (mistakenly billed as Eddie Lambert). Eugene was a young man when he appeared with the Boys in 1953. The act consisted of Eugene walking on stage with a large well-worn suitcase. From the suitcase came the sound of someone trying to get out. Eventually Eugene took his character Frankie, a puppet he had made himself, out from the suitcase and what followed could only be described as magical, with singing and joking as Frankie asked "which one of us is the dummy?" The hilarious closing part of the act had Eugene battling with Frankie as he resisted getting back into the suitcase. Hilarious is an understatement and I speak from personal experience as I witnessed the very same act being performed at the occasion of the 2007 European Sons of the Desert Convention in Dublin at which Eugene was a special guest. Frankie had retired at this stage with Finnegan replacing him.

Eugene related the story of his experience that night back in 1953. He was quite nervous as he was a relative newcomer to the stage. Born in the West of Ireland, he was making a name for himself in the difficult world of show business when he received a call for a charity show with Laurel and Hardy. Although quite confident with his performances, he was shaking on this particular occasion as watching from the wings was none other than Oliver Hardy himself. Eugene was aware of his presence from the start as he explained, **"Ollie watched every act from the side of the stage that night."**

In an interview for the 2007 convention Eugene said, **"I was finishing my act and going through the part where I put Frankie back into the suitcase. Frankie was arguing and fighting and as I closed the case and leaned back up, I hit Hardy on his belly. I froze for a second and he simply smiled at me. I went to the centre of the stage and took my bow but felt very embarrassed by it. When the show finished that night I went looking for him to apologise and found him getting autographs from the other performers. I approached him and apologised for hitting him. He was so gracious and understanding and told me not to worry, that he had enjoyed the act so much and was probably standing too close to the stage anyway. He told me that if he was ever to go solo, he would love an act like mine. Then he asked for my autograph and asked me to come upstairs to have some tea. Of course I was not going to say no and I followed him up to a small room where Stan was lying on a couch wrapped up in a large,** oversized fur coat. He apologised for not getting up, explaining that he had a bad cold and was not feeling too good. Both their wives were there and were extremely pleasant and such lovely people. We had tea and cakes. More buns than cakes which I enjoyed. What I absolutely treasure to this day was the twenty or so minutes I spent with them."

Eugene went on to become one of Ireland's most popular children's entertainers. His television show Wanderly Wagon ran for fifteen years and he opened his own puppet theatre and puppet museum in Dublin. He was so gracious with his time that the Jitterbugs Tent of Ireland even held a Tent meeting in his puppet theatre.

Eugene's wife May told me that his appearance at the 2007 Convention was a huge highlight for him and he loved talking to the Sons of the Desert, signing autographs and having his photo taken. She said it had brought back so many memories of his stage days.

Eugene and Finnegan, Frankie's replacement. Euro Convention 2007 in Dublin. Author's collection

Eugene and Finnegan. Euro Convention 2007 in Dublin. Author's collection.

Finally Laurel and Hardy came to the stage with their first ever performance of "Birds of a Feather". The scenery that was being made in Belfast was not sent to Dublin for this performance and instead was making its way over to the U.K. in time for its opening night there. So the Boys went on stage alone and improvised their routine using props from the Olympia's selection. A plain black backdrop was used.

The sketch consisted of Stan and Ollie meeting outside a pub. They keep missing each other by coming and going through two separate doors. When they eventually meet, Stan tells Ollie that he has found an opening that might suit them, as whisky tasters. The incentive is, the more you drink, the more you get paid. However, they no sooner take the job and overdo things leaving Ollie ending up in hospital having tried to fly out of a window!

Enter a doctor, a nurse (a man in drag), and an undertaker with confusion as to who the patient is. Stan has brought some eggs for Ollie but the nurse thinks that he has laid them. The Boys are fed some birdseed and end up walking about the stage clucking like chickens. Finally the doctor opens up a bedside cabinet and two pigeons fly out. The sketch ends with Stan and Ollie singing "Trail of the Lonesome Pine" to rapturous applause.

A report in the Evening Herald the next day stated, **"The affection in which Laurel and Hardy are held by young and old was very much in evidence in the premier of their new playlet. This latest effort, which they will present during their forthcoming tour of Britain, sticks closely to the formula that has served them so well over the years. It provides straight forward knock-about fun and the two comedians worked with their usual earnestness and to the great delight of the audience."**

Jitterbugs Ireland Tent member Neville Wiltshire writes about the joy of "Finding Pure Gold amongst the Gravel."

"As one of the oldest members of the Society of Irish Magicians it has been my sad task on several occasions to sort out the accumulated items of deceased members whose relatives would not know anything about our craft.

One of these friends was Eustace Malcolm, retired ESB photographer who died in his mid-80s from the detrimental effects of falling out of a tree he was trimming with a chainsaw.

Amongst his possessions were about seventy envelopes of black and white 35mm negatives, over 1800 pictures of the activities of the society from 1947 to 1968. Some of these were labeled and dated but some were not. I have had these for years as it was impossible to recognise faces from a small negative and printing them would have been too expensive.

Technology develops and I eventually found a reasonably priced device to turn the negatives into positive digitally stored pictures so I could sort them out. More tedious than difficult it backs up a project of mine to place the records of the society in the National Theatre Archives of Ireland.

One set was marked "Magician, Ventriloquist etc. Olympia".

The magician was one I knew well as Neil Phelan and the ventriloquist was a young Eugene Lambert. I reckoned it was in the early 1950's as Eugene's dummy was the one he made himself when he was a teenager. Then on the very last frame was a negative of two figures. Turning this into a positive print— UNBELIEVABLY— it was Stan Laurel and Oliver Hardy."

These pictures that Neville had were taken at the charity concert. It shows the Boys in the first photograph of them performing Birds of a Feather. Strictly copyright to Neville Wiltshire

Eustace had been at the theatre to take photographs for the Magician's Society that night, in particular Neil Phelan. The following photograph was also taken on the afternoon of October 11th 1953 and shows Neil as he performed his classic magician's act as warm up for Stan and Ollie. It was taken from the side of the stage possibly from the viewpoint of Oliver Hardy.

**Neil Phelan performing at the Olympia Theatre 11th Oct 1952.
Photograph courtesy of Neville Wiltshire with strict conditions.
Photographer Eustace Malcolm.**

Another photograph existed from that afternoon and it is of Eugene Lambert and Frankie. Again my thanks go to Neville Wiltshire for these amazing discoveries which surely would have been lost forever were it not for Neville's interest in Irish theatre and preserving history. All three photographs are now safely in the hands of the theatre archives.

Eugene's photograph was taken from the front of the stage and shows the young ventriloquist plying his craft with Frankie and suitcase in tow.

Eugene Lambert and Frankie, Olympia Theatre October 11th 1953. Courtesy of Neville Wiltshire, with strict conditions. Photographer Eustace Malcolm.

Having performed their new sketch to a live audience and receiving the applause they had hoped for, the Boys returned to the Royal Marine Hotel and began packing. Their time in Ireland had come to an end and they were ready to embark on the tour of Britain that had been planned for them. On the 12th October they boarded the "Princess Maud" at Dun Laoghaire and sailed away from Ireland for the last time leaving many happy boys and girls who would always remember meeting these two comedians.

Tales would be told for many years about "the time I met Laurel and Hardy", and smiles would appear at the mere mention of their names. Without doubt, Stan and Oliver left a legacy and an impression not only on the world but on the Emerald Isle that is still talked about today.

Above, the Boys on stage in Britain showing the backdrop that was made in Belfast and used for "Birds of a Feather". Norwich Hippodrome 1954.

The tour continued into 1954 right up to the 17th May at the Palace Theatre in Plymouth. They were due to play a week's engagement but after only one night that had to be cancelled. Oliver Hardy had been taken ill with a high temperature and was receiving treatment. Ordered to rest completely, he was confined to his hotel where he made a slight recovery. Stan was approached about going on alone but would not hear of it. **"I would not attempt it. It would have been disappointing. I am lost without Hardy."** They did not know it, but they had played their last show.

Oliver was diagnosed with having a mild heart attack and as a result Stan made arrangements for their journey home a few days later. On 30th May they checked into the Royal Station Hotel in Hull and on June 3rd they boarded the "Manchuria" completely unnoticed and sailed for home.

Much has been written about the final years of Laurel and Hardy and it is catalogued elsewhere in readily available books and online articles. The two giant pioneers of comedy duos ended their days in comfortable surroundings, with their family present in their lives.

The legacy they left is the stuff of another book perhaps. They have been analysed and copied and have influenced arguably more comedians than any other. The simple, innocent humour that they gave the world is endearing to audiences of all ages and is something that has now sadly disappeared. To say we will never see their like again is indeed true. We will not!

Laurel and Hardy films exist in all formats and are easily bought or watched on other media platforms for new audiences to enjoy and hopefully this will continue for many years to come because what the world needs more of, is Laurel and Hardy.

Oliver Hardy

The death of Oliver Hardy, that Falstaffian recipient of innumerable slings, arrows, and custard pies, will be mourned by two or three generations of those lucky people who remember films when comedians were truly comic.

In Dublin, Hardy's death is particularly regretted by Leo McCabe and Stanley Illsley of the Olympia Theatre. Hardy and his partner, Stan Laurel, came to Dublin in 1952. They came back in the following year, and used the Olympia as a rehearsal house for six weeks, living in the Royal Marine Hotel at Dun Laoghaire.

"They both liked Ireland enormously," said Leo McCabe, "and everybody they met here liked them. Hardy, who was known, absurdly enough, as 'Babe' to his friends, was the chum of every point-duty policeman in Dublin. He got into plenty of trouble about parking, but once he pushed that harassed ball of lard that was his face out of the window and pleaded with the law, he was always excused."

Oliver Hardy, photographed in Dublin during his visit here a few years ago. (See "An Irishman's Diary").

Above, an obituary for Oliver Hardy from a Dublin newspaper in which Leo McCabe appears to recall an incident with a Dublin policeman.

Jean Darling

A publication such as this would not be complete without mention of Jean Darling. One of the original "Our Gang" members who filmed their funny antics at the Hal Roach studio. Jean remembered her mother taking her to work at the studio when she was a young child and Stan being ever much the gentleman with her, to the point of flirting. Stan loved joking around with all the Our Gang kids and Jean told how he taught her to carve balsam wood. She had a role in the Laurel and Hardy film "Babes in Toyland, although uncredited.

When her Our Gang days ended she went on to a career in singing and landed the role of Carrie in the original Broadway production of Carousel in 1945.

She hosted her own TV show for NBC in New York, "A Date with Jean Darling". In 1974 she moved to North Circular Road in Dublin and began writing stories. She had numerous published in "The Alfred Hitchcock Mystery Magazine". But to a generation of Irish children she will always be our "Aunty Poppy" who came onto our television screens each afternoon and told us wonderful tales involving woodland animals, scarecrows and farmyard adventures. Aunty Poppy's books and cassette tapes were much sought after items and Jean loved every minute of it.

She told me many years later that she was saddened when the Aunty Poppy series was cancelled but she understood that time moved on and children wanted different types of stories and that Aunty Poppy had become dated.

She came to one of the first Jitterbugs Ireland Tent meetings and was delighted to be with us and talk about "The Boys", as she liked to call them. She was generous enough to ask about my children and came loaded with Aunty Poppy items for them, signed and given with a smile.

Jean Darling far right, with the rest of Our Gang and the Boys, on the Hal Roach lot.

Jean was a guest of honour at the Sons of the Desert European Convention in Dublin in 2007 and loved nothing better than being the centre of attention and talking about her days at the Roach Studios. When she accepted the invitation to come and join us for the event she told me in no uncertain terms that she would attend but only if I arranged her transport which I was delighted to do. She explained that if someone wanted to applaud her for something she did many years ago, they would have to organise it for her. However, if she was to be applauded for something she had done the day before, she would gladly organise things herself.

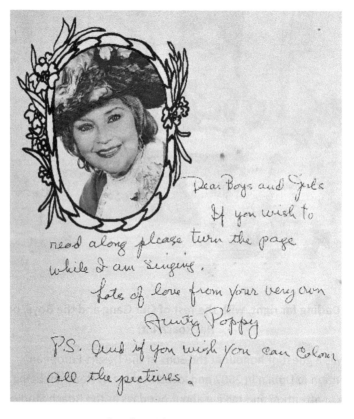

An example of Jean's work as Aunty Poppy.

As the years passed Jean continued to be invited to and attend Conventions all over Europe and delegates were always pleased to see her and talk to her.

She took little convincing to get in front of the camera once more and she took the part in her final silent film, The Butler's Tale, produced by Son of the Desert, Rene Riva in 2013.

Her mobility decreased and as she grew older she took the descision to sell her home in South Circular Road and move to Germany to be cared for by her son. She died there on September 4th 2015 and so ended a final link to the early silent films at the Hal Roach Studios

**Above, an example of Jean's Aunty Poppy books.
Courtesy of Emma Muldowney**

Oliver Hardy's Irish Roots?

As quoted from The Irish Press, on page 60 Oliver Hardy desperately wanted to get to the Genealogical Office in Dublin. His passage had been impeded many times due to traffic stopping autograph hunters. His mission, to try to find out where his grandmother Mary Tomkin was from. He never made it to the records office and so wasn't able to fulfil his wish. So was May Tomkin of Irish descent?

We know from a previous trip to Edinburgh that Oliver had asked a professor at the university there to trace his lineage as he was convinced he came from Scottish and Irish blood. He loved these islands so much that perhaps he desperately wanted to believe he was from here. Mary Tomkin did actually exist. She was his maternal great grandmother. Did she come from Ireland? The probabilities are sadly, virtually nil.

Mary Tompkins Owensby was born c.1800 to Samuel Owensby and Sally Tompkins. Her birthplace is unknown but it is most likely New York. I'm convinced it is not Ireland by the fact that her father Samuel was born in 1763 in Westchester New York. Samuel married Sally Tomkins who was also from a Westchester family. The likelihood that this family chose to come to Ireland in the late 1700s is nearly impossible.

Mary and her parents moved to Edgefield County South Carolina and there she met Wiley Freeman. They married and had a daughter Mary in 1835. Mary Freeman would eventually marry Thomas Benjamin Norvell and these were Oliver Hardy's grandparents.

Sadly Mary Tompkins Owensby's story didn't have a happy ending. The following is an account of her death and my thanks to T. Dowling for the information.

The deceased said to a witness on the evening before the morning of her death, "Mr. Freeman has killed me," and to another about the same time, "I am dead, Mr. Freeman has killed me." The prisoner, after his arrest, upon being interrogated why he had killed his wife, replied, "Because I loved her?" and said further, "I killed her because she loved another better than me." To a fellow prisoner in jail, he said, "he had killed her, but if it was to do again, he would not do it." These declarations by the deceased, and admissions of the prisoner. Held admissible in evidence. - The State v. Wiley Freeman, 1 Speers' R., p. 57. (1843.) Before Earle J., at Edgefield, Fall Term, 1842.

The prisoner was indicted for the murder of Mary Freeman, his wife, from who he had been separated more than a year. She lived in Edgefield, he in a neighbouring county in Georgia. The prisoner, on being arraigned, informed the court that he would be ready for trial on a later day in the term. When brought up for trial, a motion was made on his behalf, to continue the case until the next succeeding term, supported by an affidavit, which will be exhibited to the court with this report. The presiding Judge overruled the motion for continuance, and ordered the trial to proceed. On the day of the death of Mary Freeman, the prisoner passed the ferry, on Savannah river, a few miles from the residence of the deceased; he was armed with a rifle, and said to the ferry-man and another, that he was going after his child, which had been stolen from him, and he intended to have it or would have blood. He crossed the river about noon, and was no more seen in the neighbourhood, but was arrested sometime after in the wilds of Baker County, Georgia. In the evening of the same day on which the prisoner crossed the ferry, several of the neighbours visited the house of the deceased. Those who first arrived, found her weltering in her own blood,

within and across the threshold mortally wounded by a rifle ball, which had passed entirely through the body. She died the next morning, when Mary Stone approached the bed on which she had been placed, and accosted her, the deceased threw her arms around the neck of her visitor and said "Mr. Freeman has killed me." Mary Stone said "I hope you will be better when the doctor comes." The deceased replied, "I shall never be any better in this world." She was then very feeble and continued to grow weaker until she died. To Nicholas Cook who saw her about the same time, she said, "I am dead, Mr. Freeman has killed me." What the deceased said to these two persons was admitted in evidence as her dying declarations. Admissions of the prisoner were likewise given in evidence against him. After his arrest in Georgia, he was asked by some one of the party, why he killed his wife? His reply was, "because I loved her." The person re-joined, that's a pretty tale, to which the prisoner made the further reply, "I killed her because she loved another better than me." After his confinement in the jail, he made a further admission to a fellow prisoner, who talked with him about the death of his wife. The prisoner said, "he had killed her, but if it was to do again, he would not do it," and seemed very sorry for what he had done. His Honor saw nothing in

the circumstances under which these admissions were made to make them inadmissible, and the objections were overruled, as were likewise the objections to the indictment. And the cause was committed to the Jury, who in a few minutes returned a verdict of guilty, and he was executed accordingly on the 17th of February, 1843, acknowledging the justness of his sentence.

Did Oliver Hardy actually believe that he was of Irish stock or was he perhaps simply giving The Irish Press something exciting to write about in order that Ireland could claim one of the world's famous comedians as their own? Did he know of Mary Tomkin and her unnecessary appalling demise and want to put her name in something of the spotlight for a brief moment? I'm of the opinion that he did quite possibly believe that his great grandmother was born in Ireland. The America that Oliver grew up in was full of Irish people and their descendants, who were running from a land that had neglected them to the new world in search of a better life. He is certain to have encountered some of them during his childhood and possibly loved their lifestyle, their resolve and their way of thinking. Perhaps his mother Miss Emmie believed it too and was told that there was Irish blood in their family. We've no way of knowing and can only speculate. One thing is for certain. When I was researching this book and was shown the newspaper article that suggested Oliver Hardy had close Irish family, I jumped around the room thinking that I'd found gold!

Wiley Freeman.

This unfortunate man, was, agreeable to his sentence, executed on Friday last, between the hours of one and two o'clock, about $1\frac{1}{2}$ miles from our village; he was accompanied to the gallows by the Rev. Mr. Kennerly, and the Rev. Mr. Reae, and a large number of citizens. After taking his stand under the gallows, Freeman addressed the spectators in a clear, distinct voice, acknowledging the justice of his sentence, and expressing a willingness to forgive all his enemies.-- *Edgefield Advertiser, 22d ult.*

The Rest of the Story

In 2003 the Neville Family from County Wexford purchased the Royal Marine Hotel and began a complete renovation and refurbishment programme. As part of this refurbishment they were delighted to name one of their new main hotel bars, "Hardy's Bar". It would be a tribute to their once famous guests and as well as that, one of the private function rooms would be known as "Laurel's Bar and Lounge".

Oliver Hardy once commented that he fell in love with Dun Laoghaire but bemoaned the fact that he could not get a decent drop of Bourbon in the place. Instead, he had the bar named after him.

The following photographs of Hardy's Bar are from the author's collection.

Members from Irish and British Tents enjoying a night in Hardy's Bar at the Royal Marine Hotel, Dun Laoghaire.

The collective leadership of Northern and Southern Irish Tents! Oh dear.

Stan Laurel and Oliver Hardy are remembered on the island of Ireland today (2019) by the Jitterbugs Tent Oasis#220, of the Sons of the Desert.

Foundered in 1999, we have sought to keep the Boys in the public eye by pushing their films into the spotlight at any possible time. Our meetings are fun filled family events that keep an ethos of fun at the centre. All are welcome.

Together with our friends in the Another Nice Mess Tent of Belfast (currently resting at the time of publication), we will continue doing this for as long as we can continue laughing.

The humour and fun that is Laurel and Hardy needs to be shared with new generations. Absolutely everyone is welcome.

www.laurelandhardy.ie

www.slapstick.ie

jitterbugs@eircom.net

The Tudor Cinema in Comber, Co. Down. One of our first venues for Jitterbugs Tent meetings. It has also been used by the Another Fine Mess Tent. A truly Irish Laurel and Hardy venue.

Irish Times September 17th 1931. "Jail Birds" was more commonly known as "Pardon Us

ODEON ★ DUNDRUM
TO-NIGHT AT 8
Laurel & Hardy in
" FRATERNALLY YOURS "
Also Lon Chaney in **" SON OF DRACULA "**
Thursday: **LESLIE HOWARD** in
" PYGMALION "
Also: **" TORNADO."** at 7.15

23rd May 1954. Fraternally Yours was also known as Sons of the Desert

Irish Times April 16th 1932. The now lost "Rogue Song" was playing.

Laurel and Hardy back in Ireland? That's what the people of Cork thought when the film stars' "doubles"—"Dump" Harris and Stan—rode along Grand Parade. It was polling day, everybody had posters out, so the two comedians decided to do their bit—for themselves.

How the Irish General Election of 1954 was seen.

"Near Dublin"—Hal Roach—Pathe

Laughs in Novelty Setting

Type of production....2 reel comedy

Regardless of the laughs in this—which are of average number—it has a novelty of setting to recommend it. As the title indicates, the scene is "near Dublin." Stan Laurel, the star, is seen as a postman in a small village in the Emerald Isle. James Finlayson is the stoney-hearted landlord who orders the girl and her old father out of their home unless either the rent or the girl is forthcoming. Heavy stress is laid on the love of the Irish for brick-throwing. There is a barn dance that ends in a free-for-all battle, and murder trial that is quite funny.

Film Daily May 4th 1924

NEAR DUBLIN: Stan Laurel—Here is something new and different in comedies, depicting rural life in Ireland. Clever, interesting and many laughable incidents. Stan, why not take a trip around the world, studio speaking, of course, and give us one from every nation. Think they would go over finely if produced with the care that this was.—Philip Rand, Rex theatre, Salmon, Idaho.—General patronage.

Exhibitors Herald 15th May 1924

"Near Dublin"
(Pathe—Comedy—Two Reels)

The newest of the series of Hal Roach two-reel comedies starring Stan Laurel is, like the majority of the preceding issues, a burlesque. This time, it is the type of romantic Irish plays such as Chauncey Olcott appears in so successfully on the speaking stage, that it travesties. Stan is cast as a postman, the rival of the village noble for the hand of a fair colleen. The nobleman is a hard-hearted villain. He has Stan jailed but he escapes and in a fight Stan makes it appear that the nobleman has killed him. Stan keeps under cover, but during the murder trial a fire breaks out and Stan appears. Everyone believes he is a ghost and they scamper away in confusion. The nobleman learns the truth and an amusing chase begins. The way the characters skip lightly away is sure to get a laugh. There is considerable slap-stick and everyone indulges in brick throwing all through the picture. While it lacks some of the snap of the previous Laurel comedies, it is nevertheless amusing and the "plot" and atmosphere are quite out of the ordinary. It should prove an amusing and entertaining offering with the majority of patrons.—C. S. S.

Moving Picture World 10th May 1924

Exhibitors Trade Review

'NEAR DUBLIN'

Pathe   2 reels

Stan Laurel makes things hum in th.s unusual comedy. The scene is an Irish village and great stress is laid on the fighting instincts of the Irish men, women and children, and bricks and clubs are as thick as taxis on Broadway. Many new stunts are introduced that make this picture one of Laurel's best.

Stan is a postman in the village and is in love with the belle of the town. His rival is a brick manufacturer, who makes bricks for both building and social purposes. Stan is thrown into jail on a trumped up charge but escapes and in a battle with his rival he is knocked out by a rap on the head. The villain is jailed and Stan wins the lady.

The scene at the barn dance is cleverly arranged and it shows what a delightful fight can be arranged with the proper setting. It is wonderul in how many different ways a brick can be used as a weapon.

The court scene is also good and brings many laughs. It is full of good clean action and funny situations.

Laurel has made some good comedies but this is by far his best. It is away from the usual run of slap-stick and makes one sit up and take notice. It will appeal to any audience. It is safe booking for any program.

* * *

Exhibitors Trade Review 10th May 1924

DUBLIN
FOR TWO WEEKS COMMENCING TUESDAY, MAY 27th, 1952.

ILLSLEY-M^cCABE

present
For the First Time in Ireland

STAN LAUREL and **OLIVER HARDY**
The World Famous Comedians

FOURPENCE

Bibliography

The Laurel and Hardy Encyclopedia, Glenn Mitchell

Stan and Ollie The Roots of Comedy, Simon Louvish

Laurel or Hardy, Rob Stone

The Laurel and Hardy Scrapbook, Jack Scagnetti

A Spot of Trouble in Southend, Roger Robinson

Infinite Variety, Dan Lowery's Music Hall, Eugene Watters and Matthew Murtagh

Laurel and Hardy, The British Tours, A.J. Marriot

The Comedy World of Stan Laurel, John McCabe

Babe, The Life of Oliver Hardy, John McCabe

From the Forties Forward, Scott MacGillivray

The Laurel and Hardy Digest, Willie McIntyre

Norman Wisdom, My Turn, Norman Wisdom with William Hall